AF553353

Dr. B.R. Ambedkar
A True Nationalist

Dr. B.R. Ambedkar
A True Nationalist

Professor (Dr.) Samrendra Sharma

Dr. B.R. Ambedkar: A True Nationalist

Edition : 2026

ISBN 978-93-87537-49-1

Published by:
CRESCENT PUBLISHING CORPORATION
4806/24, Mathur Lane,
Ansari Road, Darya Ganj,
New Delhi - 110 002
Ph.: 011 - 23244131
Mob.: + 91 - 9711991838, 9999021668
E-mail: crescentbook@gmail.com
Website: www.crescentpublishingcorp.weebly.com

Printed at:
Roshan Offset Printers
Delhi

Acknowledgements

Dr. B.R. Ambedkar is perhaps the most read, appreciated, criticised and followed person in modern Indian History.Writing anything about him was a big challange which I feel could be taken up with the help of my advocate friends with whom I used to discuss intricacies of different laws prevailingly in India and ultimately got fascinated towards the life and works of Dr. B.R . Ambedkar made the most elaborated constitution of India. Most prominent among them is Sh. Kulbhushan Manhas former President Bar Association and a leading lawyer cum social worker of this region. My special thanks to him as he remained a constant source of inspiration during writing of this book.

Secondly I must thank my colleagues in the deprtments of English, Political science and History who arranged for all the books forme from market and otherwise and made me read them to prepare a vast background of B.R. Ambedkar to deal with him as a leader of the nation.

My son Dr. Rakesh Sharma, during the writing of this book, discussed with me how Dr. Ambedkar turned towards Buddhism in the last period of his life and why did he do so to keep his national spirit intact. I am thankful to him for igniting my desire to write a book on Ambedkar as a true nationalist.

I am thankful to all the political parties and social organisations in India which keep Dr. B.R. Ambedkar as an ideal in one way or the other and thus compelled a person like me to delve deep into the life and works of this great man.

I am thankful to the publisher Crescent Publishing Corporation, Darya Ganj, New Delhi.

Preface

Ambedkar's legacy as a socio-political reformer, had a deep effect on modern India. In post-Independence India, his socio-political thought is respected across the political spectrum. His initiatives have influenced various spheres of life and transformed the way India today looks at socio-economic policies, education and affirmative action through socio-economic and legal incentives. His reputation as a scholar led to his appointment as free India's first law minister, and chairman of the committee for drafting the constitution. He passionately believed in individual freedom and criticised caste society. His accusations of Hinduism as being the foundation of the caste system made him controversial and unpopular among Hindus. His conversion to Buddhism sparked a revival in interest in Buddhist philosophy in India and abroad. Many public institutions are named in his honour, and the Dr. Babasaheb Ambedkar International Airport in Nagpur, otherwise known as Sonegaon Airport. Dr. B. R. Ambedkar National Institute of Technology, Jalandhar, Ambedkar University Delhi is also named in his honour. Ambedkar's political philosophy has given rise to a large number of political parties, publications and workers' unions that remain active across India, especially in Maharashtra. Ambedkar was a prolific student, earning doctorates in economics from both Columbia University and the London School of Economics, and gained a reputation as a scholar for his research in law, economics and political science.[3] In his early career he was an economist, professor, and lawyer. His later life was marked by his political activities; he became involved in campaigning and negotiations for India's independence, publishing journals, advocating political rights and social freedom for Dalits, and contributing significantly to the establishment of the state of India. In 1956 he converted to Buddhism, initiating mass conversions of Dalits. Ambedkar's legacy as a socio-political reformer, had a deep effect on modern India. In post-Independence India, his socio-political thought is respected across the political spectrum. His initiatives have influenced various spheres of life and transformed the way India today looks at socio-economic policies, education and affirmative action through socio-economic and legal incentives. His reputation as a scholar led to his appointment as free India's first law minister, and chairman of the committee for drafting the constitution. He passionately believed in individual freedom and criticised caste society. His accusations of Hinduism as being the foundation of the caste system made him controversial and unpopular among Hindus Several movies, plays, and other works have been based on the life and thoughts of Ambedkar.

Contents

FORMATIVE INFLUENCES ON AMBEDKAR'S PERSONALITY

Chapter 1

PSYCHOLOGICAL TREATMENT OF DR. B.R. AMBEDKAR'S PERSONALITY

The prime objective of here is to the present research paper is to study and understand the personality of Dr. Ambedkar with the help of psychological concepts and terminology. It is indeed a huge task but the researcher has made a valid attempt to understand and explain Ambedkar. Nearly negligible research is conducted on Ambedkar and psychology. Dr. Ambedkar was a great intellectual on international repute, with knowledge of various subjects and fields. All of his higher education was completed in foreign countries in reputed universities and acclaimed professors. The professors helped him to widen his scope regarding education and to apply it to society in the means of changing it and not only understanding the society.He was a true academician and a true citizen of India who utilized and applied all his degrees, knowledge, experience and wisdom for the development of his country.

Personality

Ambedkar at Columbia University was especially influenced by two of his professors: John Dewey (the initiator of pragmatic philosophy) and R.A. Seligman, the eminent economist. He was also inspired by Booker T. Washington, the founder of Tuskegee Institute who promoted education as a means of African, American emancipation. Being and learning with above mentioned great scholars made Ambedkar s personality with a blend of conscientiousness, extrovertion and self-actualization. Conscientiousness personality individual is organized, thorough, planful and efficient. Extroversion personality is assertive, active, energetic and talkative. A self-actualized person realizes his highest potentials. The research found all the three together in Ambedkar.

Insight Learning

Learning is any relatively permanent change in the behaviour.Insight learning helps an individual to use in core intelligence and his own perceptions for solving facing the problems of his life with the available resources. Ambedkar has used many times his insight in his life for the dalits and for the development of education in the country. Dr. Ambedkar view was to use the educational resources to the most extent by pooling system. His suggestion regarding pooling system was, insteadof engaging many teachers of higher education of the same subject at different colleges in a particular city, theses teachers in a particular subject should work together as a homogenous group. He believed that the available resource (teachers) to reach the masses instead of only confined to a particular college for the rest of life. It will not only help the student but we could able to produce professoriate adequate to deal with both under-graduate and post-graduate work.

Locus of Control

Locus of control is whether your actions and cognitions are controlled by self or by others. In precise whether your are dependent on the people and situations or your independent to take yours own decisions. There are two types of locus of control, internal and external. Dr. Ambedkar had internal locus of control therefore he was independent in his thinking and decisions, did not get disturbed by others reactions and opinions and being self motivated. It is because of his self motivation he availed, utilized and successfully completed all the opportunities he received during his education in the foreign countries. He believed and followed the personality style of being open to experience. These experiences make you learn the practicalsessions of what the theories have taught you.

Rational thinking

Dr. Ambedkar was of pragmatic approach instead of idealistic. He gave importance to science &technology courses. He also established „BhartiyaSamajSevaSangh whose motto was to read, read out, and hear, understand, realize and give realization. He was of opinion that education can provide self-respect and dignity. He also thought that curriculums vision should be prepared in such a way so that it develops rationality among learners. Rationality tends to give the capacity to distinguish truth from untruth. He believed that religious behvaiour should be based on thinking or else it has no importance.

Character, values and principles

The three principles inherited from his master Gautambuddha. They are Pradnya (knowledge), Sheel (wisdom), and Karuna (compassion). He gave lot of importance to these three principles and tried to imbibe them in masses. As being professor Dr. Ambedkar hated if somebody asked for favour to give passing marks. He never compromised his principles and always presented his views in a studied manner with proper research evidence and support.DrAmbedkar denied power but never denied his principles.Ambedkar thought that character along with education can help the individual to utilize his knowledge for the development and development of human civilization and culture and develop his own personality. He observed "An educated man without character and humility is more dangerous than a beast. If his education is detrimental to the welfare of the poor, the educated man is curse to society.... character is more important than education".

Leadership Style

A Benevolent autocrat is a leader who knows what he wants from the people; situation and how to get things competed in his way without resentment. In the present investigation the researcher foundDr. Ambedkarwas a benevolent autocrat leader, who knew what he has to do for India and the downtrodden caste. To achieve this objective his education helped him completely.All the above if you need to lead the masses you should be equipped with the best education and whatbetter to have it from the best universities of the world. He not only gained

Assertiveness

Dr Ambedkar had the courage to handle and write on the issues of annihilation of caste, untouchables who they were and how they became untouchables, which were avoided by some leaders of that time. Dr. Ambedkarhad impact of his master Gautam Buddha andSantKabir and later Mahatma Phule. Due to his masters teaching and principles hisbehaviour was very balanced and controlled. He knew not to react but respond to people and situations.The researcher found him cool, calm and collected manner using his assertiveness and wisdom. He was also assertive in making changes in the admission register of private institutions providing primary or secondary schools to strictly prohibit in mentioning the caste and sub cast of students.

Ambedkar encouraged people to take higher education for their progress of self and community.He believed in giving academic autonomy to teachers to frame their own syllabi and opposed to rigid structure syllabus. He not only founded Peoples Education society in 1945 but also opened night high schools, hostels and colleges.

Eleanor Zelliot stated that Ambedkar developed a strong belief in democratic institutions to bring about social equality and these ideas were large passed on to him by John Dewey. Dewey s emphasis was on education a means of not only understanding but means to change it. Ambedkar considered education as the basis of social, economic and political revolution.

Chapter 2

Dr. B.R.AMBEDKAR AND HIS VISION FOR RECONSTRUCTION OF INDIAN SOCIETY

Babasahab Dr.Bhimrao Ramji Ambedkar belongs to the rare class of great men who set standards of greatness for themselves and live up to them. In his own words "a great man must be motivated by the dynamics of social purpose and must act as a scourge and scavenger of the society." His life itself stands as a testimony to this ideal of securing human dignity to all. He avouched the mission of his life by proclaiming that "For the protection of human rights several great men have immolated themselves at the altar of duty. Better to die in the prime of youth for a great cause than to live like an oak and do nothing." Dr.Ambedkar embodied a peerless personage among all the national leaders who only had the moral propriety to assert that "I am a man of character." He waged a valiant struggle against the "diabolical contrivance to suppress and enslave humanity" -the Brahmanical system to make the subhuman and servile majority regain their human personality through social, economic, political and cultural emancipation. He declared that "Our battle is for Freedom. Our battle is not for few economic and political gains. Our battle is for the reclamation of Human Personality which was suppressed and mutilated..."

The range of Ambedkar's struggle for securing human dignity is very vast. He had to start from the Right to be Human to attain highest humane level. Dr.Ambedkar's ideas, writings and outlook could well be characterized as belonging to that trend of thought called *Social Humanism*. He developed a socio-ethical philosophy and steadfastly stood for human dignity and freedom, socio-economic justice, material prosperity and spiritual discipline. His name will glitter forever in the firmament of world history not only as a great social philosopher but also as a great revolutionary who dedicated his entire life for the amelioration of the teeming millions of the underdogs.

Academic training and social commitment

Ambedkar was thoroughly influenced by two illustrious personalities- Lord Buddha and John Dewey. Amidst scores of philosophers postulating on human misery, Buddha stands tall for his radical epistimo - psychological breakthrough shifting from substance thinking to process thinking. Instead of engaging in abstract speculation about the extraterrestrial origins and purposes of the universe and human existence, Buddha called for an empirical investigation into the actual conditions. Explaining the causal origination of the Brahminical society and the conditions in creating and maintaining a society as 'Alpajana sukhaya', Buddha sets out to reconstitute an equitable and harmonious society of 'Bahujana sukhaya' by rearranging the socio-economic and political relations grounded on morality. Ambedkar, following Buddha questions the determination of social position based on innate nature. He explains that the Bahujans are the victims in this schema of *Colonization of mind and capturing social order*.

It is pertinent to note here that Ambedkar considers Buddha as a victim of the Brahmanical society, "Oppressed by the evils and misery then prevalent in the Aryan Society he renounced the world. Dr.Ambedkar found that the central message of the life of Buddha is reconstructing that Brahminical philosophy and society in the light of scientific enquiry, which he proclaims as the historic rebellion of Gautama Buddha.

He came under the influence of the outstanding American philosopher of the time, Prof.John Dewey at the Columbia University. Dewey had forsaken the then dominant Hegelian theory of ideas, and *formulated an instrumentalist theory of knowledge, which conceived ideas as instruments to solve social problems.* Ambedkar internalized Dewey's message, which considered philosophy, in its essentials, as criticism involving reconstruction. Ambedkar's teacher of public finance, Edwin R A Seligman who was then the professor of political economy at Columbia was firmly placed among the most outstanding students of public finance and history of economic thought at that time and when Ambedkar went to London, his teacher was an equally eminent economist, Edwin Cannan who was also an acknowledged authority on the history of economic thought.Even during his student days Ambedkar in 1918 reviewed Bertrand Russell's work, 'The Principles of Social Reconstruction' and finds his thesis is shaky. Applying Russell's ideas to Indian society, he observes "Thus it is not survival but the quality, the plane of survival that is important. If the Indian readers of Mr. Russell probe into the quality of their survival and not remain contented merely with having survived I feel confident that they will be convinced of the necessity of a revaluation of their values of life.

Dr.Ambedkar's thought has a view very much different from capitalist or communist view, or the Eastern or Western thought. It is a genuine interaction between Western liberalism and Indian reality as he experienced it and theoretically comprehended it. On the philosophical plane, he was rooted in *Buddhist dialectics, in reason and science.* On the socio-economic and political level, his ideas were grounded in the principle of *socialist democracy.* He had a definite agrarian programme and industrial strategy. He had a dream to enrich democracy. In his economic writings, Dr.Ambedkar made a blistering attack on the imperial economic policy and exploitation. Many professors in London felt that the view expressed by Dr.Ambedkar in his paper on "Responsibilities of a Responsible Government in India" and other works were of a revolutionary nature.

On the question of relationship between the polity and the economy, Ambedkar held a more complex view than ether Liberalism or Marxism. He postulated two superstructures upon the structure of society – the economy and the polity. Of the two superstructures, Ambedkar gave relatively greater weight to the economy than to polity, and that was why he found himself, despite obvious differences, close to Marxism .Unlike Marx, Ambedkar does not see the possibility of statelessness, while he does want castelessness first in India and later, classlessness.

Ambedkar's exhumation of 'Society' in India:

Dr.Ambedkar held that there were two qualitatively different groups which had not only been historically central, but continued to be central, to social organization and social dynamics. These were caste and class. Historically, the Vedic Varna system, which was a class order, had been transformed into a caste order subsequently, and in modern India the nascent class order was continually and complexly distorted and defeated by caste order. This is the point of his challenge to Marxists when he asked them whether the Indian proletariat, caste-fragmented, can ever become a class in itself, let alone a class for itself. He explained with diligence that the formation of caste society, coupled with gender inequity is to safeguard the interests of the Brahminical groups in relation to other groups, maintain their moral and mental control over them, and preserve their position of power, prestige and privilege.

Denial of Existential Dignity

Ambedkar explained that the Brahaminical system denies the right to existential dignity to the Bahujans and relegates them a subhuman existence As a consequence, they are denied three essential rights, viz., their *right to Identity*. All the identities that are attached to the Bahujans are not given by themselves, but are called by others. The identities like Anarya, Pisacha, Sudra, Atisudra, names of individual castes and even the surnames-all are insulting, demeaning identities and are the identities of suppression. The Bahujans are denied the *right to Choice of Occupation* and are forced to take up polluting occupations as hereditary occupations. "There are many occupations in India which on account of the fact that they are regarded as degraded by the Hindus provoke those who are engaged in it to aversion... all are slaves of the caste system. But all slaves are not equal in status". They are forbidden to exercise any *right to Access or Claim over Resources* of the society in which they live. On the whole, the caste system clamps social oppression, economic exploitation and political suppression which are worse than slavery

Mechanism and Perpetuation

Castes are divided into different classes of castes. A Hindu is caste consciousas well as class conscious. *Whether he is caste conscious or class conscious depends upon the caste with which he comes in conflict.* If the caste with which he comes in conflict is a caste within the class to which he belongs, he is caste conscious. If the caste is outside the class to which he belongs, he is class conscious. The basic weakness of the Hindu social order is that it does not recognize the individual as the centre of social purpose, for it is based primarily on caste and not on individuals. There is no room for individual merit and no consideration of individual justice. Rights, privileges and disabilities and duties are based on the caste to which the individual belongs. It can be understood from the analysis of Ambedkar that Brahmanical ideology as an *ideology of exclusion* which moulded a social order based on inequality where no two castes are equal and the divided castes are made to oppose each other.

Enforced Poverty and Cultural Capital

Dr.Ambedkar is the first social scientist to find out several facets of dehumanization in the caste system, powered through the engine of religion. Before Dr.Ambedkar several attempts were made to paint caste as only a social aberration. The Hindus are the only people in the world whose economic order - the relation of workman to workman is consecrated by religion and made sacred, eternal and inviolate. The graded inequality puts the classes on a vertical plane not merely through conventions but through spiritual, moral and legal structure.

Ambedkar defined culture as a more fundamental category in which both politics and economics intersected. His diligent exposition of the economics of Brahmanism as the *law of enforced poverty* based on the *dogma of predestination*, conditioning the victims as willful vassals reveals the *third dimension of capital, i.e the Cultural Capital.*While economic capital refers to the command over economic resources, social capital relates to the resources based on group membership, relationships, networks of influence and support. Cultural Capital on the other hand, concerns forms of knowledge, skills and advantages that confer power and higher status in the society. Culture shares many of the properties that are characteristic of economic capital that *any 'competence' becomes a capital in so far as it facilitates appropriation and unequal distribution thereby creating opportunities for exclusive advantage to individuals or groups in the society.* Ambedkar presented an elaborate illustration of such cultural advantages which are monopolized by the twice-born and are used to condition the behaviour and attitudes of the servile castes for the social, economic and political dominance of the leisure castes. He was the first to trace out the relation between Brahamnical ideology, caste system and economic exploitation. These notions were comprehensively developed later into the concept of Cultural Capital. *"To sum up, the Brahmin enslaves the mind and the Bania enslaves the Body"* paralyses and cripples the people from helpful activity.

The Necessity of Social Transformation

In India, he analyses that there is no society at all. We have multitudes of societies based on caste. People are not born as humans. They are born into castes and imbibe such notions of mind which do not allow humane interaction among them. "The first and foremost thing that must be recognized is that Hindu Society is a myth… In every Hindu the consciousness that exists is the consciousness of caste. That is the reason why the Hindus cannot be said to form a society or a nation" .He explains the ethnocentric belief that the Hindu Social System has been perfected for all times has prevented the *reconstruction of the Hindu Society* and stood in the way of a revision of vested rights for the common good.He squarely blames "Brahmanism in instituting caste system has put the greatest impediment against the growth of nationalism" ."Unless the social order is changed, no progress could be achieved. The community cannot be mobilized either for defense or for offence. Nothing can be built on the foundations of caste. No nation, no morality".

Annihilation of caste- notional change

Ambedkar was thoroughly convinced that unless a casteless and classless society is created there will be no progress in India. This requires a social reconstruction and Ambedkar was very clear about the means to bring about this change. Ambedkar took up the reconstruction of Indian society on the foundations of democracy as a 'mode of associated living.' He asserted that Democracy, properly understood and applied would only be the panacea and initiated his public life in1916 on this cause.

Differing with the Congress and other 'Nationalists', he declared that social revolution must precede political revolution so as to ensure that every citizen enjoy the benefits of political freedom."That political reform cannot with impunity take precedence over social reform in the sense of *reconstruction of society*...". He reinstates his position that the worth of independence depends on the kind of government and the kind of society that is built up. "Indeed the vision of a New Order in a New India would very greatly strengthen determination to win freedom". Exposing the Jatpat Todak Mandal which aspired to '*Remodel Hindu Society*', Ambedkar stressed that '*Reconstitution of the society*' by annihilating caste and its ideological notions is the cure(the low castes in to Citizens of equality. In Ambedkar's discourse, Nation is a power-homogenized fraternity and a democratic unity. He strived for Nation, as a new social formation characterized by a consciousness of unity and fraternity leading to increased, intensified non-discriminate social exchanges.

Ambedkar's Actions for Social Transformation

Dr.Ambedkar in his grand scheme of reconstruction of Indian society, fought for rights of representation as democratic rights. Basing on the prorata of population, he reasoned that all sections of the society including women should get rights of representation spheres of education, employment, agriculture, industry, bureaucracy and governance of this country. Branding that the Brahmanical society is based on *Culture of Reservations*-keeping education, rule and economy reserved 100% for the Brahmanical castes and relegating the Bahujans to service, he wanted to usher in Democratic society based on the *Culture of Representations*. His memoranda to the Southborough Committee, Montague-Chemsfeld committee, Muddiman Committee and his arguments in Round Table Conferences are based on the rights of representation as democratic rights.

Assertion and Equal Citizenship

Babasaheb Ambedkar debunked all those reforms that question only the traditions but never intended to debase the ideological foundations of those customs as '**sectional reforms**' rather than '**social reforms**'. It was during the Mahad Satyagraha in 1927 that the 'aim' of the movement was proclaimed by Dr.Ambedkar as, "*not only removing our own disabilities, but also at bringing about a social revolution that will remove all man-made barriers of caste by providing equal opportunities to all to rise to the highest position and making no distinction between man and man so for as civic rights are concerned*". While the Mahad Satyagraha focused on 'social & legal equality' the Kalaram Temple Satyagraha focused on 'religious equality'. The Charter *of Right and Demands* of that Dr.Ambedkar presented before the *Indian Statutory Commission* commonly known as *Simon Commission* had a wider '*constitutional significance*' for equal citizenship. While all the participants at the Round Table Conferences were busy with their Communal Representations (Hindu,Muslim,Sikh, Parsi etc.) it was only Dr.Ambedkar who raised the issues of Civic equality, Adult Franchise and Citizenship to all Indians.

Away from the Brahminism

The Conversion conference of 1936 enshrined the philosophy of 'human beings' and the ideology of democratic revolution comprehending not only Social, legal & civic equality but also religious equality. This event is significant that it helped members of the society to realize the necessity to understand that religion no longer be inherited but be examined rationally by everybody. It also is a deliberate attempt to debase the Brahminical culture that employ religion as the engine of oppression. Dr. Ambedkarremarked that if the bottom- most stone in a structure is shifted, those above it are bound to be shaken out of their position .

The movement from 1936 entered a new phase for attaining 'economic equality' along with social, legal, civil & religious equality, by the abolition of caste & class, considering both Brahmanism and capitalism as necessary evils. The formation of 'Independent labour Party' was a new experiment to formulate the government of 'labouring classes' who also happen to be the exploited castes in Indian social system. He held the view that ills were not due to machinery and modern civilization; they were due to *wrong social organization* which had made private property and pursuit of personal gain matters of absolute sanctity.

These equalities were to be achieved in the trinity of 'liberty, equality and fraternity' by Constitutional rights and guarantees, and much more significantly by the reconstruction of society based on this trinity principle. It was due to his thoughts on the above subjects which enabled a Constitutional scheme of Government of India Act, 1935 much ahead of democratic Constitution of Independent India.

Blueprint for a society- Constitution

Contempory Constitutional authority, Granville Austin has described the Constitution of India as 'first and foremost a social document with three broad objectives-ensuing unity, democracy and creating a social revolution. "The majority of India's Constitutional provisions are either directly arrived at furthering the aim of social revolution or attempt to foster this revolution by establishing conditions necessary for its achievement."

The Constitution of India bears the impression of Dr.Ambedkar's thought as a key instrument for National Reconstruction. He was the lone speaker at the Constituent

Assembly of 1946, which discussed the frame work of future Constitution to underline the need to build up a cohesive society. *"Our difficulty is how to make the heterogeneous mass that we have today take a decision in common and march on the way which leads us to unity. Our difficulty is not with regard to the ultimate; our difficulty is with regard to the beginning"*. In order to establish an inclusive society, Ambedkar looks at democracy, not as a political arrangement, but as "a mode of associated living. The roots of democracy are to be searched in social relationship, in terms of the associated life between the people who form the society" (Keer, 1962:480). He highlights fraternity as the root of democracy and without fraternity other ideals of democracy like equality and liberty cannot endure. He defined democracy as a "form and method of government where by revolutionary changes in the economic and social life of the people are brought about without bloodshed" (Keer, 1962:61).

The Constitution of India, in order to reconstitute the society on the democratic foundations of equality, liberty, fraternity and justice, incorporated legislations for equality and equal opportunity in all spheres of life. Road map is laid for a democratic and inclusive society through reservations as representations. In order to create social polarization among the victims of the Brahmanical social system, Ambedkar engineered the category *'Backward classes'* would cover three principal components, the Scheduled Castes, the Scheduled Tribes and the Other Backward classes. And he addressed himself to the task of securing social justice for all the Socially and Educationally Backward Classes in the country, under the mandate of a new constitution. It is to be underlined that the *Idea* is to break monopoly by proportional representations, *Policy*- is to Bring SC,ST, OBC on one platform in order to Break caste system as representations are for collection of castes, not for individual castes-as Backward classes.

The Directive Principles strive to create a Welfare State and a just social order. Making the State responsible for social change, Article 38 contains the essence of these principles: "The State shall strive to promote the welfare of the people by securing and protecting as effectively as it may a *social order* in which justice-social, economic and political -shall inform all the institutions of national life". He announced that the people of India "Expect to happen in a sovereign and free India is a complete destruction of Brahminism as a philosophy of life and as a social order".

Ambedkar identified the functioning of moral order, observance of Constitutional morality as the conditions for the successful working of democracy. "Society must have either the sanction of law or the sanction of morality to hold it together without either, society is sure to go to pieces".

Buddhism for establishing Moral Society and New Social Order

Ambedkar found the means to develop essential social and moral conscience of the society for establishing democratic society in Buddhism. He holds that the essence of Buddhism consists not in the removal of suffering- which is only negative and incidental, but in the attainment of perfection, which is positive and fundamental - i.e. establishing a democratic society. He declared his mission to make India as *Prabuddha Bharat,* an Enlightened India.

New Identity, New Personality and New Social order

A Buddhist is an identity of an individual who is liberated from the bondage of dogma, an interrogator of the sources of oppression, a self consciously liberal and secular in world view. Dr. Ambedkar calls for a change in the personality of a Buddhist based on the ideals of *Pradgna, Sila* and *Karuna*- Competence, Character and Compassion, which he himself has embodied. He exhorts that Morality is not passive; it is pro active. To defend democracy, in its true sense, becomes the moral duty of every Buddhist.

Incompatibility of Ideologies and continuing contradictions

The cherished aspiration of paving way for an inclusive society has not yet been realized, reasons too well known for Ambedkar.

The unmitigated contradictions of our society have resulted in a situation that the laws are on the side of equality, and the customs that people follow in their daily lives are on the side of inequality.(*From Dowry to several forms of corruption, Caste violence and Gender violence etc.,*) This paradox is explained as the incompatibility of ideologies. "Indians today are governed by two different ideologies. Their political ideal set out in the preamble of the Constitution affirms a life of liberty, equality and fraternity. Their social ideal embodied in their religion denies them" He warned that "political democracy cannot succeed where there is no social and economic democracy"

India Today

It is unfortunate that even after six decades of Constitutional policy, democratic ideals are yet to find firm ground among the citizens of India. Owing to illiteracy, poverty and powerlessness they are not in a position to make democracy work. The Fundamental rights provided to the Socially and Educationally Backward Classes in Article 15 and 16 of the Constitution, who constitute the majority i.e., Bahujans of the country, are being denied to a large extent in the pretext of dubious argument of merit(*Fundamental Rights to Enabling Provisions*). This equal opportunity legislation quite often drives the society to take emotional polemic positions (*forum for justice!*). The underlying problem is that method has been confused with the policy. Providing representations or fair access or equal opportunity being the policy, the quota mechanism is a method to secure fairness. (Thorat, 2008). In addition, Ambedkar's practical policy of bringing unity among the Socially and Educationally Backward Classes on the basis of their common victimhood (Scheduled Castes due to untouchability, Scheduled Tribes on the basis of isolation and Other Backward Castes who are socially and educationally deprived) as the platform of unity has been ignored, even by the victims of caste system themselves. It is because they still continue to be influenced by the ideology of exclusion, Brahminism which shapes their lives.

Ambedkarism as a way to the World

Hence, it is the responsibility of the civil society especially the educated sections to create social and moral consciousness and build a humane society. In an important way, Dr.Ambedkar thus gave expression to an inner need in India for a just social condition; on such basis alone can National well-being be secured. Though mindful of the great obstacles to the establishment of democratic arrangement in Indian society, Ambedkar was optimistic about a cohesive society. "I am convinced that, given time and circumstances, nothing in the world will prevent this country from becoming one and with all our castes and creeds, I have not the slightest hesitation in saying that we shall in some way be a united people" He exhorted the nation to preserve independence by establishing equality and fraternity in all spheres of life. World requires to be reconstructed for the public good, common good and universal good of humankind. Ambedkarism shows the way-out. It has a vision to build up a 'New World'.

Chapter 3

OPPOSITION TO UNTOUCHABILITY

As Ambedkar was educated by the Princely State of Baroda, he was bound to serve it. He was appointed Military Secretary to the Gaikwad but had to quit in a short time. He described the incident in his autobiography, *Waiting for a Visa*. Thereafter, he tried to find ways to make a living for his growing family. He worked as a private tutor, as an accountant, and established an investment consulting business, but it failed when his clients learned that he was an untouchable. In 1918, he became Professor of Political Economy in the Sydenham College of Commerce and Economics in Mumbai. Although he was successful with the students, other professors objected to his sharing a drinking-water jug with them.

Ambedkar had been invited to testify before the Southborough Committee, which was preparing the Government of India Act 1919. At this hearing, Ambedkar argued for creating separate electorates and reservations for untouchables and other religious communities.In 1920, he began the publication of the weekly *Mooknayak* (*Leader of the Silent*) in Mumbai with the help of Shahu of Kolhapur i.e. Shahu IV (1874–1922).

Ambedkar went on to work as a legal professional. In 1926, he successfully defended three non-Brahmin leaders who had accused the Brahmin community of ruining India and were then subsequently sued for libel. Dhananjay Keer notes that "The victory was resounding, both socially and individually, for the clients and the Doctor."

While practising law in the Bombay High Court, he tried to promote education to untouchables and uplift them. His first organised attempt was his establishment of the central institution Bahishkrit Hitakarini Sabha, intended to promote education and socio-economic improvement, as well as the welfare of "outcastes", at the time referred to as depressed classes.For the defence of Dalit rights, he started five periodicals – *Mooknayak* (the leader of the dumb, 1920), *Bahishkrit Bharat* (Ostracized India, 1924), *Samta* (Equality, 1928), *Janata* (The People, 1930), and *Prabuddha Bharat* (Enlightened India, 1956).He was appointed to the Bombay Presidency Committee to work with the all-European Simon Commission in 1925.This commission had sparked great protests across India, and while its report was ignored by most Indians, Ambedkar himself wrote a separate set of recommendations for the future Constitution of India.By 1927, Ambedkar had decided to launch active movements against untouchability. He began with public movements and marches to open up public drinking water resources. He also began a struggle for the right to enter Hindu temples. He led a *satyagraha* in Mahad to fight for the right of the untouchable community to draw water from the main water tank of the town.In a conference in late 1927, Ambedkar publicly condemned the classic Hindu text, the Manusmriti (Laws of Manu), for ideologically justifying caste discrimination and "untouchability", and he ceremonially burned copies of the ancient text. On 25 December 1927, he led thousands of followers to burn copies of Manusmrti.Thus annually 25 December is celebrated as *Manusmriti Dahan Din* (Manusmriti Burning Day) by Ambedkarites and Dalits.

In 1930, Ambedkar launched Kalaram Temple movement after three months of preparation. About 15,000 volunteers assembled at Kalaram Temple satygraha making one of the greatest processions of Nashik. The procession was headed by a military band, a batch of scouts, women and men walked in discipline, order and determination to see the god for the first time. When they reached to gate, the gates were closed by Brahmin authorities

Poona Pact

In 1932, British announced the formation of a separate electorate for "Depressed Classes" in the Communal Award. Gandhi fiercely opposed a separate electorate for untouchables, saying he feared that such an arrangement would divide the Hindu community.Gandhi protested by fasting while imprisoned in the Yerwada Central Jail of Poona. Following the fast, Congress politicians and activists such as Madan Mohan Malaviya and Palwankar Baloo organised joint meetings with Ambedkar and his supporters at Yerwada.On 25 September 1932, the agreement known as Poona Pact was signed between Ambedkar (on behalf of the depressed classes among Hindus) and Madan Mohan Malaviya (on behalf of the other Hindus). The agreement gave reserved seats for the depressed classes in the Provisional legislatures, within the general electorate. Due to the pact, the depressed class received 148 seats in the legislature, instead of the 71 as allocated in the Communal Award earlier proposed by British Prime Minister Ramsay MacDonald. The text uses the term "Depressed Classes" to denote Untouchables among Hindus who were later called Scheduled Castes and Scheduled Tribes under India Act 1935, and the later Indian Constitution of 1950.In the Poona Pact, a unified electorate was in principle formed, but primary and secondary elections allowed Untouchables in practice to choose their own candidates.

Political career

Ambedkar's political career started in 1926 and he continued to hold various positions in the political field until 1956. In December 1926, the Governor of Bombay nominated him as a member of the Bombay Legislative Council; he took his duties seriously, and often delivered speeches on economic matters. He was a member of the Bombay Legislative Council until 1936.In 1935, Ambedkar was appointed principal of the Government Law College, Bombay, a position he held for two years. He also served as the chairman of Governing body of Ramjas College, University of Delhi, after the death of its founder, Rai Kedarnath. Settling in Bombay (today called Mumbai), Ambedkar oversaw the construction of a house Rajgruha, and stocked his personal library with more than 50,000 books. His wife Ramabai died after a long illness the same year. It had been her long-standing wish to go on a pilgrimage to Pandharpur, but Ambedkar had refused to let her go, telling her that he would create a new Pandharpur for her instead of Hinduism's Pandharpur which treated them as untouchables. At the Yeola Conversion Conference on 13 October in Nasik, Ambedkar announced his intention to convert to a different religion and exhorted his followers to leave Hinduism. He would repeat his message at many public meetings across India.

A photograph of the election manifesto of the All India Scheduled Caste Federation, the party founded by Ambedkar, 1946

Ambedkar published his book *Annihilation of Caste* on 15 May 1936. It strongly criticised Hindu orthodox religious leaders and the caste system in general, and included "a rebuke of Gandhi" on the subject. Later, in a 1955 BBC interview, he accused Gandhi of writing in opposition of the caste system in English language papers while writing in support of it in Gujarati language papers.

In 1936, Ambedkar founded the Independent Labour Party, which contested the 1937 Bombay election to the Central Legislative Assembly for the 13 reserved and 4 general seats, and secured 11 and 3 seats respectively. Ambedkar was elected to the Bombay Legislative Assembly as a legislator (MLA). He was a member of the Assembly until 1942 and during this time he also served as the Leader of the Opposition in the Bombay Legislative Assembly.All India Scheduled Castes Federation was a socio-political organisation founded by Ambedkar in 1942 to campaign for the rights of the Dalit community. During the year 1942 to 1946, Ambedkar served on the Defence Advisory Committee and the Viceroy's Executive Council as minister for labour.

After the Lahore resolution (1940) of the Muslim League demanding Pakistan, Ambedkar wrote a 400-page tract titled *Thoughts on Pakistan,* which analysed the concept of "Pakistan" in all its aspects. Ambedkar argued that the Hindus should concede Pakistan to the Muslims. He proposed that the provincial boundaries of Punjab and Bengal should be redrawn to separate the Muslim and non-Muslim majority parts. He thought the Muslims could have no objection to redrawing provincial boundaries. If they did, they did not quite "understand the nature of their own demand". Scholar Venkat Dhulipala states that *Thoughts on Pakistan* "rocked Indian politics for a decade". It determined the course of dialogue between the Muslim League and the Indian National Congress, paving the way for the Partition of India.

In his work *Who Were the Shudras?,* Ambedkar tried to explain the formation of untouchables. He saw Shudras and Ati Shudras who form the lowest caste in the ritual hierarchy of the caste system, as separate from Untouchables. Ambedkar oversaw the transformation of his political party into the Scheduled Castes Federation, although it performed poorly in the 1946 elections for Constituent Assembly of India. Later he was elected into the constituent assembly of Bengal where Muslim League was in power. Ambedkar contested in the Bombay North first Indian General Election of 1952, but lost to his former assistant and Congress Party candidate Narayan Sadoba Kajrolkar, who polled

138,137 votes compared to Ambedkar's 123,576. He tried to enter Lok Sabha again in the by-election of 1954 from Bhandara, but he placed third (the Congress Party won). By the time of the second general election in 1957, Ambedkar had died.

Ambedkar had twice became a member of the Parliament of India representing Bombay State in the Rajya Sabha, the upper house of the Indian parliament. His first term as a Rajya Sabha member was between 3 April 1952 and 2 April 1956, and his second term was to be held from 3 April 1956 to 2 April 1962, but before the expiry of the term, he died on 6 December 1956.On 30 September 1956, Ambedkar had announced the establishment of the "Republican Party of India" by dismissing the "Scheduled Castes Federation", but before the formation of the party, he passed away on 6 December 1956. After that, his followers and activists planned to form this party. A meeting of the Presidency was held at Nagpur on 1 October 1957 to establish the party. At this meeting, N. Sivaraj, Yashwant Ambedkar, P. T. Borale, A. G. Pawar, Datta Katti, D. A. Rupavate were present. The Republican Party of India was formed on 3 October 1957. N. Shivraj was elected as the President of the party.

Drafting India's Constitution

Upon India's independence on 15 August 1947, the new Congress-led government invited Ambedkar to serve as the nation's first Law and Justice Minister, which he accepted. On

Ambedkar, chairman of the Drafting Committee, presenting the final draft of the Indian Constitution to Rajendra Prasad on 25 November 1949

29 August, he was appointed Chairman of the Constitution Drafting Committee, and was appointed by the Constituent Assembly to write India's new Constitution.

Ambedkar was a wise constitutional expert, he had studied the constitutions of about 60 countries. Ambedkar is recognised as the "Father of the Constitution of India". the Constitution Assembly, a member of the drafting committee, T. T. Krishnamachari said, "(...) it happened ultimately that the burden of drafting this constitution fell on Dr. Ambedkar and I have no doubt that we are grateful to him for having achieved this task in a manner which is undoubtedly commendable." Granville Austin described the Indian Constitution drafted by Ambedkar as 'first and foremost a social document'. 'The majority of India's constitutional provisions are either directly arrived at furthering the aim of social revolution or attempt to foster this revolution by establishing conditions necessary for its achievement.' The text prepared by Ambedkar provided constitutional guarantees and protections for a wide range of civil liberties for individual citizens, including freedom of religion, the abolition of untouchability, and the outlawing of all forms of discrimination. Ambedkar argued for extensive economic and social rights for women, and won the Assembly's support for introducing a system of reservations of jobs in the civil services, schools and colleges for members of scheduled castes and scheduled tribes and Other Backward Class, a system akin to affirmative action. India's lawmakers hoped to eradicate the socio-economic inequalities and lack of opportunities for India's depressed classes through these measures. The Constitution was adopted on 26 November 1949 by the Constituent Assembly.

Opposition to Article 370

Members of the Bharatiya Janata Party state that Ambedkar opposed Article 370 of the Constitution of India, which granted special status to the State of Jammu and Kashmir, and it was included in the constitution against his wishes. Ambedkarite scholar Pratik Tembhurne points out that this attribution emerged for the first time in a Rashtriya Swayamsevak Sangh publication *Tarun Bharat* in 1991, four decades after Ambedkar's death. Its veracity is not confirmed. According to Dhananjay Veer's biography, when asked in a press conference whether Article 370 helped solve the problem of Kashmir, he responded that it was unfair on the part of Kashmir to expect India to provide military and other necessary services but to not merge with it.

Support for uniform civil code

I personally do not understand why religion should be given this vast, expansive jurisdiction, so as to cover the whole of life and to prevent the legislature from encroaching upon that field. After all, what are we having this liberty for? We are having this liberty in order to reform our social system, which is so full of inequities, discriminations and other things, which conflict with our fundamental rights.

During the debates in the Constituent Assembly, Ambedkar demonstrated his will to reform Indian society by recommending the adoption of a Uniform Civil Code. Ambedkar resigned from the cabinet in 1951, when parliament stalled his draft of the Hindu Code Bill, which sought to enshrine gender equality in the laws of inheritance and marriage

Economic planning

Ambedkar was the first Indian to pursue a doctorate in economics abroad. He argued that industrialisation and agricultural growth could enhance the Indian economy. He stressed investment in agriculture as the primary industry of India. According to Sharad Pawar, Ambedkar's vision helped the government to achieve its food security goal. Ambedkar advocated national economic and social development, stressing education, public hygiene, community health, residential facilities as the basic amenities. He calculated the loss of development caused by British rule.

Conversion to Buddhism

On October 13th, 1935 Ambedkar presided over the Yeola Conversion Conference, held in Yeola, in Nasikh District. He advised the Depressed Classes to abandon all agitation for temple-entry privileges; instead, they should leave Hinduism entirely and embrace another religion. He vowed, "I solemnly assure you that I will not die as a Hindu." Ambedkar considered converting to Sikhism, which encouraged opposition to oppression and so appealed to leaders of scheduled castes. But after meeting with Sikh leaders, he concluded that he might get "second-rate" Sikh status, as described by scholar Stephen P. Cohen.

Instead, he studied Buddhism all his life. Around 1950, he devoted his attention to Buddhism and travelled to Ceylon (now Sri Lanka) to attend a meeting of the World Fellowship of Buddhists. While dedicating a new Buddhist vihara near Pune, Ambedkar announced he was writing a book on Buddhism, and that when it was finished, he would formally convert to Buddhism. He twice visited Burma in 1954; the second time to attend the third conference of the World Fellowship of Buddhists in Rangoon. In 1955, he founded the Bharatiya Bauddha Mahasabha, or the Buddhist Society of India. He completed his final work, *The Buddha and His Dhamma,* in 1956 which was published posthumously.

After meetings with the Sri Lankan Buddhist monk Hammalawa Saddhatissa, Ambedkar organised a formal public ceremony for himself and his supporters in Deekshabhoomi, Nagpur on 14 October 1956. Accepting the Three Refuges and Five Precepts from a Buddhist monk Mahasthavir Chandramani in the traditional manner, Ambedkar completed his own conversion, along with his wife. He then proceeded to convert some 500,000 of his supporters who were gathered around him. He prescribed the 22 Vows for these converts, after the Three Jewels and Five Precepts. On this occasion, many upper caste Hindus too accepted Buddhism. After Nagpur, on 16 October 1956, Ambedkar again gave Buddhism to more than 300,000 of his followers at Chandrapur, since the place is also known as Deekshabhoomi. He then travelled to Kathmandu, Nepal to attend the Fourth World Buddhist Conference. There he went to the Dalit settlements of Kathmandu city, and saw the condition of Nepali Dalits, he was visibly angry. When this matter became known to the then Prime Minister of Nepal Tanka Prasad Acharya, then the Prime Minister himself came to Sheetal Niwas (guest house and Rastrapati Bhawan of Nepal), where Ambedkar stayed and assured Ambedkar that due attention will be given to improving the condition of the Dalits. Ambedkar had called for the Dalits of Nepal to start their struggle to get their rights. The Nepali Ambedkarite movement is run by Dalit leaders, and most of the Dalit leaders of Nepal convinced that "Ambedkar's philosophy" (*Ambedkarism*) is only the way to get rid of caste-based discrimination. His work on *The Buddha or Karl Marx* and "Revolution and counter-revolution in ancient India" remained incomplete.

Influence and legacy

Ambedkar's legacy as a socio-political reformer, had a deep effect on modern India. post-Independence India, his socio-political thought is respected across the political spectrum. His initiatives have influenced various spheres of life and transformed the way India today looks at socio-economic policies, education and affirmative action through socio-economic and legal incentives. His reputation as a scholar led to his appointment as free India's first law minister, and chairman of the committee for drafting the constitution. He passionately believed in individual freedom and criticised caste society. His accusations of Hinduism as being the foundation of the caste system made him controversial and unpopular among conventional Hindus. His conversion to Buddhism sparked a revival in interest in Buddhist philosophy in India and abroad.

Ambedkar's political philosophy has given rise to a large number of political parties, publications and workers' unions that remain active across India, especially in Maharashtra. His promotion of Buddhism has rejuvenated interest in Buddhist philosophy among sections of population in India. Mass conversion ceremonies have been organised in modern times, emulating Ambedkar's Nagpur ceremony of 1956. Followers of the Navayana regard him as a bodhisattva, the Maitreya, although he never claimed it himself. Outside India, during the late 1990s, some Hungarian Romani people drew parallels between their own situation and that of the downtrodden people in India and converted to Buddhism. Japan's Burakumin community leaders are spreading the Ambedkar's philosophy to the Burakumin people. For his actions towards the salvation and equality of mankind, his followers and the Indian people started respectfully addressing him as "Dr. Babasaheb Ambedkar", since sometime between September–October 1927. "Babasaheb" is a Marathi phrase which roughly translates, literally as "Father-Sir" (baba: father; and saheb: Sir) or "Respected Father" because millions of Indians consider him a "great liberator".Ambedkar is also known as "Bhim". This name is used for many things like Bhim Janmabhoomi (*birthplace of Bhim*). Bhim Jayanti (*birthday of Bhim*), Jai Bhim (*victory to Bhim*), Bhim Stambh (*Bhim pillar*), Bhim Geet (*Bhim song*), Bhim flag, Bhim Army, Bhim Nagar, BHIM, Bhim Sainik (*Bhim soldier*), Bhim Garjana etc. *Jai Bhim* is a greeting used by Ambedkarites, followers of Ambedkarism.

Statues and monument commemorating Ambedkar are widespread throughout India, as well as existing elsewhere. Many public institutions are named in his honour, such as the Dr. Babasaheb Ambedkar International Airport, Dr. Ambedkar International Award, Dr. B. R. Ambedkar National Institute of Technology, Jalandhar, and Ambedkar University Delhi. A large official portrait of Ambedkar is on display in the Indian Parliament building. Ambedkar was voted "the Greatest Indian" in 2012 by a poll organised by History TV18 and CNN IBN. Nearly 20 million votes were cast. The first Prime Minister of India, Jawaharlal Nehru said that, "Dr. Babasaheb Ambedkar was a symbol of revolt against all oppressive features of the Hindu society." In 2004, Columbia University honors Ambedkar in the course of its 250th birthday celebration. The University also referred him as "the founding father of modern India".

The Maharashtra government acquired the house in London where Ambedkar lived during his days as a student in the 1920s. In 2015, the house was converted into a museum-cum-memorial named Dr. Bhimrao Ramji Ambedkar Memorial.The Government of India is preserving or developing five sites associated with Ambedkar as 'Panchtirtha'. Ambedkar's Panchtirtha are: Bhim Janmabhoomi (place of birth), Deekshabhoomi (land of Buddhism accepted), Statue of Equality (Mumbai), Dr. Bhimrao Ramji Ambedkar Memorial (London), and Dr. Ambedkar National Memorial (Mahaparinirvan Bhoomi of Delhi). A proposal to build a grand memorial called Statue of Equality or "Dr. Babasaheb Ambedkar Memorial" was approved in 2015 to be located in Mumbai. Since that time, other tall statues of Ambedkar have been announced for places such as Amravati (*Dr. B. R. Ambedkar Memorial Park,* 125 ft) and Hyderabad.

THOUGHT ON DALIT WOMEN

The Indian society, like most of the other societies in the world, is a complex social structure consisting of a number of social phenomena such as caste, gender, ethnicity and class. Caste, as a sociological construct, is not a universal phenomenon and is relevant only to the Indian society. On the contrary, gender as an omnipresent phenomenon has a strong bearing on the social formation on the basis of the relations between the two opposite sexes. Most of the times, these relations are identical with the binary of power and subordination, marginalisation.

The ideas of caste and gender are so intertwined in the Indian social structure that one cannot sufficiently understand the status and position of women in Indian society without reference to the category of caste as overbearing factor in almost all areas or regions of the country. The identity of individual is not denoted by the qualities he possesses but by the caste, which he belongs to. The history of women in the Indian social context is prominently related to the emergence of caste and the place of women in the caste structure. The status of women in India has been a historical record of subordination and marginalisation granted by the socio-cultural-religious system. Subject to many changes that occurred from last some millenniums, the condition and the role of women has been constantly shifting since the time of *Shastras,*

Smritis and *Vedas.* During pre-independence period, two movements which affected the position of women were Social Reform Movement initiated in the19th century and the Nationalist Movement in the 20th century. Among all the social reformers and humanists who worked during this period for the upliftment and empowerment of Indian women, Dr. Babasaheb Ambedkar was one who strongly felt the need of education to women. Jyotiba Phule s women s liberation movement enormously inspired Dr. Ambedkar. Liberation of women was taken up by him as the main part of renaissance. According to him, women must be liberated from their oppressive conditions. His tough struggle was to liberate women from the age-old slavery and to create their share in all the spheres of life. As an architect of the Indian constitution, he strictly mentioned in his article entitled *The Rise and Fall of Hindu Woman* that the root-cause of suffering for women in India may be attributed to the so-called Hindu religious books. A book like the *Manusmriti* divides people into a stratified caste system and promotes inequality between men and women. According to the *Manusmriti,* women have no right to education, independence, or wealth. While *Manusmriti* enslaved women, Dr. Ambedkar awakened their minds, ignited their hearts, strengthened their energies and resurrected them as powerful human beings. He fought against the state and society to realise justice for women.

In the 19th century, Raja Rammohan Roy and other social reformers engaged with the problems of women. They tried to build up positive public opinion on the issues like widow remarriage, custom of sati and child marriage, etc. Their approach, however, was paternalistic and caste bound. Dr. Ambedkar, while commenting on the precedence of political reform to social reform in India, argues that social reform in India was the reform of Hindu families and not the reorganisation of other society. The social reformist failed to remove evils such as forced widowhood, sati, etc. which prevailed among them. Dr. B. R. Ambedkar not only championed the cause of social awakening and justice for the deprived, downtrodden and unprivileged sections of the Indian society but also worked tirelessly throughout his life to challenge the authority of orthodox Hindu social order that upheld unjust gender relations in an institutionalised manner. In his journey from the claim of equality and justice for the untouchables to his conversion to Buddhism, Ambedkar gave an ear to the voice of the Dalit women, who are triply exploited in the patriarchal caste hegemonic Hindu society. Starting from his efforts to eradicate untouchability, he was keen to understand the Dalit women s critical conditions. Exposed to the western ideas of humanism and rational thinking, he was appalled at the low status of women in the Hindu society. He not only worked hard at the grassroots level to raise awareness about the degraded status of women in India but also wrote extensively to counter the views on gender relations sanctioned by the Shastras and upheld by Hindu religious tradition. According to him, women should be considered as women first and then a wife and a mother. His ideas of the liberation of women, particularly Dalit women, were more powerful than those of the champions of women s liberation movement all over the world. He was of the firm belief that unless the women themselves came forward to fight against the discrimination and exploitation, no outside agencies would change their condition. The book like *Manusmriti* deplores the condition of women forever. It is found difficult to come out of the societal web that has created around women by religious scriptures and books. For him, the deplorable condition of women and the inhumanity imposed upon them by the Hindu society is so not only because they belong to the opposite sex but because they belong to lower caste. Therefore, the question of women cannot be isolated from the question of caste. He attacked the institution of caste which he felt opposed to the basic human values. The fundamental principle of Hindu social order is „graded inequality . To quote him,

That the principle of graded inequality is a fundamental principle beyond controversy. The four classes are not on horizontal plane, different but equal. They are on a vertical plane, not only different but unequal in status, one standing above the other. In the scheme of Manu, the Brahmin

is placed at the first in rank. Below him is the Kshatriya. Below the Kshatriya is the Vaishya. Below Vaishya is the Shudra and below Shudra is the Atishudra or the untouchable.[1] Below the four tiers of the Hindu social order was the women s class who possessed humble position in the caste hierarchy. Shudra was the lowest according to caste hierarchy but Dalit woman was lower than the lowest according to caste and gender as well.

He, in fact realised the need to change the Hindu society radically. He challenged the notion of women as incomplete human beings. The *Pothi*, the *Puranas* and the religious scriptures held women as parasites, whose existence depends upon the mercy of her master. Dr. Ambedkar rejected this view and denounced the idea that women were parasites. To him, individual is the ultimate goal of society and all-round growth of an individual is the most important pre-requisite of a free social order. Unfortunately, Hindu religion gives little importance to the individuality and values its member on the basis of certain Varna or Caste. His mission in life was to reconstruct Hindu society along the modern democratic ideas of liberty, equality and fraternity.

According to Dr.Ambedkar her sufferings are two-fold: she has her own share of universal suffering as a woman and additionally, she is the victim of a variety of exploitations such as social, religious, economic, and cultural as a Dalit woman. Her experience of patriarchal domination is qualitative, more severe than that of a non-Dalit woman. Furthermore, opportunities and avenues available to her for voicing her grievances and agonies are very few. Marginalisation of low caste was legitimised by religious sanction. This sanction was achieved by implementing the dominant ideology in the cultural and other institutions of the society and transmitting to the succeeding generations by cultivating among them the appropriate patterns of thought and behaviour. The cultural marginalisation of Dalit women was cultivated among them by their fear to challenge the Hindu social order. In his speech at the gathering of women at the Mahad satyagrah, Dr. Ambedkar articulated the linkage between caste and gender. In directing the attention of Dalit women to specificities of women s subordination by caste, he underlined the simultaneity of their subordination as Dalits and as women. Dr. Ambedkar asked them to give up their excessive metal jewellery and dress pattern that were both public markers of the Brahminical class and gender code. For women, who preserve caste and boundaries between castes, dropping of the markers suggests an assertion against the Brahminical code and intra-caste patriarchy. to quote him:

Learn to live in cleanliness, stay away from all bad habits and vices .Give education to your children; create a sense of ambition in them. Instil in their minds the feeling that they will become great. Do not press them to marry until they have attained the capacity to bear the responsibility that comes with marriage. Those who marry should remember that it is wrong to produce many children. Even if no facilities are available to you, mothers and fathers have a responsibility to keep their children in a good condition. Every girl who marries must be ready to stand by her husband's party. Not as his slave but in a relation of equality, as his friend. If you behave according to this advice you will lift up not only yourselves but Dalit society as well, and increase respect for yourselves and for the community.[2]

The ills and the evils Dalit women suffered from were ignorance, poverty, illiteracy, blind beliefs and extreme labour. Along with that the social system and the religious sanctions for their defenseless place forced them to suffer ceaselessly. According to Dr. Ambedkar:

Dalit women possess more physical and mental stamina than Brahmin women. They should feel the power to fight with their own life and must discard the old and disgusting customs. In his speech and meeting he insisted that Dalit women must give up all the things that enable people to recognize them as being untouchable. In his words, to quote, ¯knowledge and learning are not for men alone. They are essential for women too...if you want to improve the next generation, you must not neglect to educate your daughter...[3]

Women s question, for him, was related to the system of organised exploitation inherent in the Hindu social order. Dr. Ambedkar recognised the power of education to put an end to this exploitation. Women s education was the central concern for him. He brought Dalit women in the socio-political movements by consciously organising conferences and arranging meetings. His aim was to give them the power of speech, to make them establish their own identity and help them realise their personality. Under the leadership of Dr. Ambedkar, the movement of the dalits and particularly movement of Dalit women acquired its importance. His leadership provided them the identity that was systematically seized from them for centuries. He had created a sense and self in the life of community that had long been caught in the snare of poverty, ignorance and superstition. His motivation for women to take part in their struggle for upliftment transformed them. He realised the fact that unless Dalit women took part in the liberation movement, there would not be fruitful change in their lives. He was very keen in identifying the problems of Dalit women.

The main objective of Dr. Ambedkar s movement was to fan the spark of a sense of identity in the minds of the untouchables and to instill in them the courage and the confidence to fight for their rights. His writings chiefly aimed at the awakening of the slumbered community as well as to warn the high caste Hindu community against the wrongs inflicted upon the depressed classes. The consciousness of the extreme vulnerability in the Brahminical caste pattern led Dalit women to create their own identity in the non-Dalit as well as Dalit community. Several women activists responded to his call and large number of women started taking part in his movement. They began to express their views in an honest and forthcoming manner. As a result of the awareness among women, women s association was established in 1928 in Bombay preceded by numerous conferences held for and by women all over Maharashtra. In 1942, the establishment of „Dalit Mahila Federation (Dalit Women s Federation) appeared as a major step towards initiating movement for their liberation. They carry the potential to fight for their identity, rights, and prestige that the upper caste and the middle class non-Dalit women are comparatively enjoying.

They are ready to challenge the cultural and social norms, which have allotted to them the lowest position in the caste hierarchy. In Dalit feminism, the emphasis is on the issues of self consciousness, reaction, rebellion, self-realisation, and self-assertion. Dalit women, devoid of all the differing circumstances, get rid of their own cocoon and trying to get their own voice and identity in the social structure. For them, the quest for freedom is the quest of prime importance. In the words of Betty Freidan:

For a woman as for a man, the need or self fulfillment, autonomy or self realisation, independence, individual actualization is as important as sexual need, serious consequences when it is thwarted. Women's problems are in this sense by product of the suppression of her basic need to grow and fulfill her potentialities of human being, potentialities of which mystique of feminist fulfillment ignore.

The Dalit and gender consciousness led them to launch social movements in India in the 1990s called „National Federation of Dalit Women and „All India Dalit Women s Forum . The establishment of these organisations proves that the issues and the concerns of Dalit women are beyond the arena of the Indian feminist movement. To put in the words of Vidyut Bhagwat

*Women from lower castes considered so lowly and degraded in life that their body was a free terrain of the colonisation.*The emergence of Dalit feminism is to free themselves from dominance of the indigenous colonizers. In this sense the Dalit feminism has different working agendas than the mainstream women s movement. It is not complimentary to the mainstream women movement; rather Dalit feminism emerged as a critique of the upper caste feminist movement in India. According to her again,

By using the term Dalit women', we are creating an imagined category. This imagining is necessary, because we hope that Dalit women in the near future will give new critical dimensions to the Indian feminist movement as well as to theDalit movement.

Dalit feminism seeks Dalit women s self identification, difference, selfconsciousness and autonomy.This difference is the record of their struggle against the marginalisation in the Indian social history.Though the post independence Indian social phenomena and the role of the constitution and women organisations have brought a significant change in the lives of women, they have not achieved complete freedom. The system has offered equal rights in every field of public sphere, but still the invisible gap between the opposite sexes is present everywhere. Still women, and particularly Dalit women are seeking to establish their identity by means of their organisations, movements, social gatherings, and so on. The cumulative effect of all these efforts is to enable every woman to live her life wholly, and fully, making Dr. Ambedkar s dream of women equality and empowerment true.

VIEWS ON ABOLITION OF CASTE SYSTEM IN INDIA

Caste is a system in which determination of position, rights and duties of an individual is done on the basis of the birth of such individual in a particular group. In other words we can say that, the status of an individual is determined by birth. Under caste system an individual is not allowed to change its status. We can say that it is a rigid form of stratification system, which restrict the mobility and distinctness of status. Due to the caste system several evil prevails in the society. Under a caste system and individual is compel to follow the caste occupation. Caste system leads to untouchability. It restricts the growth of brotherhood among people and also it hold off national unity and create obstacles to social progress. Caste system denies equal rights of individual, that why it is considered as undemocratic. For eradicating the problems of caste system many steps were taken by various leaders such as Mahatma Gandhi, Jyotiba Phule and the most significant role was played by Dr. B R Ambedkar. According to him for eradication of caste, it is necessary to break the religious notion on which caste system is laid down. He is of the view that caste system is not merely division of labour perhaps; it is also a division of labourers. Equality should be for all and though the success shared by all. Instead of thinking about one single community there should be a deep cultural unity of all community.

In 16th century the word caste was derived from the Spanish and Portuguese word Casta, which means race or lineage. Caste system is an example of rigid social inequality from the perspective of social organization and system of values. So far as social organization of caste is concerned, there is division of society into groups ranking in a different hierarchy and in a system of values, caste provide legitimacy to the concept of social inequality among the masses as well as give importance to the idea of purity and pollution. The roots of Hindu caste system were already in place between 1000 and 1500 B.C. When the Aryans settled near the Indus river valley. The Rig Veda a sacred text from the period describe four main Varna in traditional Hindu society : Brahmanas ; the class of priests and teachers ; Kshatriyas, the warrior class who were the rulers and soldiers ; Vaishyas, the commercial class of artisans, traders and cultivators and Shudras; the servant and peasant class.

The word caste signifies breed, race and rank which came into use for the first time in 1563 A.D. by Gracia De Orta wrote - no one can changes from his father's trade and all those of the same caste of the shoe maker are the same. To Hindu, however, the concept of caste has a narrower and more precise meaning, referring to the smaller sub-groups defined by subtle distinction of birth, intermarriage and occupation. The four Varna's described in Rig Veda comprises more than 2000 sub castes .Beneath these caste is a fifth population group- those without any caste, literally, outcastes. They are treated as Untouchables. The Indian Constitution of 1950 made untouchability illegal. Today these people call themselves Dalits (oppressed) .

In India Caste System consists of two different concepts that is Varna and Jati, the real concept of Varna has almost disappeared in the present context and has changed into Jati. The former was based on color of the skin and later on birth. It is the religious and social institution of Hindu peoples who comprised about 80% of India's population. The rest of India is Muslim, Christian, Sikh, Jain or Buddhist. Caste is such a deep rooted and pervasive concept, it is a rigid form of stratification system, in which mobility of rank and status is not allowed. However, that it has also influenced Muslims, Christians and Sikhs, for instance, they have separate churches for dalits and non dalits Christians. The 50 million Indians who live in tribal community predate the Aryan and Dravidian civilization. They are members of backward classes, they are not the part of Hindu society even then, they have started observing untouchability towards Dalits- who themselves have a caste hierarchy.

ORIGIN OF CASTE SYSTEM

Although, it is difficult to establish as to when the caste system originated, but there is no doubt that the institution of caste for the convenience of the ruling class leading to successful administration by them. There are different theories about the establishment of the caste system. These are Religious mystical, Biological, Socio-historical theories.

Religious Theory

The religious theory explained how the four Varna's were founded, but they do not explained how the Jaats in each Varna or the untouchables were founded. According to Rig Veda, the ancient Hindu book, the primal man- Purush - destroyed himself to create human society. The different Varnas were created from different part of his bodies. The Brahmans were created from his Head; the kshtriyas from his Hands; the Vaishyas from his Thighs and the Shudras from his Feet. Other religious theory claims that the Varna's were created from the body organs of Brahma, who is the creator of the world. According to Iravati Krave : the four rank system was creation of ruling class which originally had a three rank system in which whatever the differences of rank all people had right to certain rituals and sacraments from birth to death.

Biological theory

The biological theories claims that all existing things, animated and in animated, inherent three qualities in different apportionment. Sattva attributes includes wisdom, intelligence, honesty, goodness, and other positive qualities. Rajas attributes includes velour, passion, pride and other passionate qualities. Tamas attributes includes dullness, stupidity. Lack of creativity and other negative qualities. According to these attributes Brahmans inherent Sattva qualities. Kshåtriyas and Vaishyas inherent Rajas qualities and Shudras inherent Tamas qualities.

In ancient India the religion had a prominent place; the king was considered the image of God. The Priest King accorded different position to different functional groups. According to Senart, like human beings food also inherent different dosage of these qualities but he explained the origin of caste system on the basis of prohibition regarding sacramental food. He holds that the followers of a particular deity considered themselves the descendants of the same ancestors and offered a particular kind of food as offering to their deity. Those who believed in the same deity considered themselves as different from those who believed in some other deity.

Socio historical theory

The socio historical theory explains the creation of the Varna, Jaats and untouchables. According to this theory the caste system begins with the arrival of Aryans in India. Before the Aryans there were other communities in India of other origins among them Negrito, Mongoloid, Austroloid and Dravidian. When the Aryans arrived in India their main contact was with the Dravidians and Austroloids. The Aryans disregarded the local culture, they begin conquering and taken control over regions in north India and at the same time pushed the local people towards the south, jungles and mountains in north India.

The Aryans organized among themselves in three groups. The first was of a warrior called Rajayana later they changed their name to kshatriya. The second group was of priest called Brahmans. The third group was of farmers and craftsmen and they were called as Vaishyas. In order to secure their status the Aryans resolved some social and religious rules which allowed only them to be the priest, warrior and the businessmen of the society. For instance: Maharashtra in West India, many think that the meaning of the name Maharashtra is great land but some claim that the name Maharashtra is derived from the Jaats called Mahar who were considered to be the original people of this region. In the caste hierarchy the dark-skinned Mahar were outcastes. The skin color was an important factor in the caste system.

The meaning of the word Varna is not class or status but skin color. In Hindu religious stories there were many wars between the good Aryans and a dark skinned demons and devils, but the real fact was that the dark skinned slaves were in fact the original residence of India, whom the Aryans coined as monsters, devils, demons and slaves.

Therefore the caste system did not come into existence all of a sudden or at a particular date. It is the result of the long process of social evolution. A number of factors played their part in the development of the present caste system enumerated as follows:

- Hereditary occupation.
- The desire of the Brahmans to keep themselves pure.
- The lack of rigid, unitary control of the state.
- The unwillingness of ruler to enforce a uniform standard of law and custom and their readiness to

recognize the worrying custom of different groups as valid.

- Believe in re-incarnation and the doctrine of karma.
- Geographical isolation of the Indian peninsula.
- Static nature of Hindu society.
- Foreign invasion and rural social structure.

All these factors conspired to encourage the formation of small groups based on petty distinction from time to time. It may however be noted that the caste system is not specifically an institution of Hindus but it is a typical Indian institution. Further caste system is not a monopoly of India it existed and still exists in many parts of the world. What is unique in the Hindu caste system is that it alone classified some groups as untouchables and unapproachable.

ISSUES RELATING TO CASTE SYSTEM

According to P.N Bose,- the caste system has acted essentially to impose that attitude of money, needed to raise men from savagery but to stop them halfway on progress.

Disintegrating factor

The caste system has literally split up the society into hundreds of hereditary caste and sub castes and encouraged a spirit of exclusiveness and class-pride, narrowed the outlook and created wide gulfs between the various sections of the community. The caste system resulted in lots of evils because of its rigid rules. It perpetuates exploitation of the economically weaker and socially inferior caste. It protects the privileged caste and thus, builds up economic discontent and social prejudices. A person born in one caste was doomed to remain in it forever, and keep check on economic and intellectual advancement and a great stumbling block in way of social reforms, because it keeps economic and intellectual opportunities confined to a certain section of the population only and denies them to other. The Shudras and untouchables had to perform all the menial tasks. They could not do anything for their own development. The worst thing is that they cannot be permitted to devote himself to any educational or scientific profession, even when they have natural aptitudes and physical and intellectual equipment for it. Worthy and capable person are prevented by caste rigors from getting their proper and rightful places, even there next generation has to follow the same rigidness of caste system, and they too remain closed slaves and bonded labors. The caste system however is guilty of just the opposite demerit. It does not make proper provision for low-born talents or high-born incompetence.

Barred to religious ties

As far as religion is concerned the lower caste people were not even allowed to touch the holy book and sacred literatures and they were devoid to enter into the temple. This problem has given scope for religious conversion. The lower caste people were getting converted into Islam and Christianity, due to the tyranny of upper caste. Along with these issues the old Hindu Law Marriage Act 1955 promotes Anuloma marriage i.e. a boy from upper caste can marry a girl from lower caste and prohibits Pratiloma marriage i.e. a girl from lower caste cannot marry a boy from upper caste. It also inflicted untold hardships on women through its insistence on practices like child marriages, prohibition of widow remarriage, seclusion of women etc. these have made the life of women miserable.

History bears testimony that the issue of caste system sanctioned privileges to a section of society who understood themselves as a superior class and at the same time it inflicted a series of disabilities on their sections which continues from generation to generation.

Contrary to Democracy

Democracy is based on principle of equality, fraternity and liberty. On the other hand the caste system is based on inequality of status and opportunities, which often creates conflict and tension in the society. It acts as an obstacle in the normal and smooth functioning of democracy. No doubt India has got political freedom but it must be the concerned of every individual that real freedom cannot be cherished without attainment of the social and the economic democracy. It is unfortunate that the Indian society is sharply divided into various caste and sub caste which acts as a barrier due to rigidity and division of the society based on caste consideration.

Perpetuates Untouchability

The caste system has condemned large groups of people to a life of degradation without any hope of redemption. It has created Untouchables, an evil that has been sapping the very vitals of the society. This untouchability is reduced to the state of natural slavery and hindered the growth of brotherhood; hold off the national unity as it disallowed any type of social intercourse. B.R Ambedkar rightly said, Untouchability of Hindus is a rare phenomenon, humanity is any other part of the earth has never experienced it. There is no such thing in any other society. Really, the tyranny is perpetuated in the name of untouchabilty are the black lesson in human culture. . According to Mahatma Gandhi, untouchability is the hate fullest expression of caste.

Hindrance in the way of Modernization

The caste system obstructs the process of Modernization as it also restricts the mental development of an individual. Modern Indian intellect is, therefore burdened with the sense of contrition over the matter. Passions overwhelmingly carry us to a position of hostility towards any compromise, and the entire caste structure placed in the docks. Despite this it cannot be said that the caste system offers a place in which any group religion or occupation can fit in as a cooperating part of the society.

BHIM RAO AMBEDKARS: VISION

Bhim Rao Ambedkar was born in December 1981 in a Mahar community, an untouchable caste of Maharashtra. His father Ramji and grandfather Maloji was in military services. He was the youngest child of his parents and was just only five when his mother died. Thereafter his aunt took care of him. He was enrolled in a local school of Satara where he had to sit on the floor and his teacher would not touch his books as because he was untouchable. Facing so many hardships in his life B R Ambedkar continued his studies and passed his matriculation. In 1913 Maharaj OF Baroda awarded scholarship to B R Ambedkar and send him to America for attaining the degree of Masters, it was for the first time in his life he was not degraded for being Mahar.

He submerged himself in the studies and obtained the Degree of M.A, PHD from the University of Columbia. There after he proceeded to London but soon Baroda government ended his scholarship and bring him back. The Maharaja of Baroda appointed him as a Secretary but here also he faced discrimination because of being Mahar. In 1917 he returned to Bombay and joined syndrome college, Bombay as a professor of political economy on a temporary basis. the social treatment of other professors were so pathetic as they all belongs to high caste even they objected that Ambedkar can't drink water from the pot reserved for the professional staff. When he started legal practice in the High Court of Judicature, Bombay. He had no money even to obtain sanad. He had joint the appellate side of the bar. The solicitor would not condensed to have any business dealing with him because of untouchability .therefore, all these circumstances forced him to be a great rebel against the Hindu orthodoxy and its discriminatory treatment to turns his mind for searching a cult where a man is not discriminated by the another man.

Dr. Ambedkar played a significant role for the upliftment of downtrodden. He was considered as messiah for suppressed class as he belongs to untouchable's community.

He experienced caste discrimination right from the childhood, that's why he raises the issues related to untouchability there are many leaders who raise their voice for the down trodden of India, but the most significant, eminent actions were taken by B R Ambedkar because he himself faced such problems ,After noticing the evils of prevailing caste system and its impacts on suppressed human being prompted founding father of the Constitution of India to create an egalitarian society wherein justice, social, economic and political right prevails which includes equality of status and opportunity may be available to everyone irrespective of caste system.

No doubt India has got political freedom and has political democracy, but it must be the concerned of everyone that real freedom cannot be cherished without attainment of social and economic democracy. It is unfortunate that the Indian society is sharply divided into various caste and sub caste which is obstacle due to rigidity segregation and division of the society based on rigid caste consideration. B R Ambedkar was impressed enough by the conduct and humanism of the great social reformers like Budhha, Kabir and Jyotiba Phule. He declared that Untouchables must leave the Hindu culture and accept another religion instead, and he himself embraced Buddhism.

Dr. Ambedkar criticized old Law books like Manusmriti and Arthshastras who showed the inferiority and bitterness towards the suppressed class. He also criticized the higher standard of Brahmans who are category above of all. The Brahmans are somehow responsible for social exploitation and the backwardness of untouchables.

Ambedkar also rejected that there were no such invasion of Aryans as mentioned in the ancient Vedic and Sanskrit literature. He argued that Shudras were not dark skinned but Shudras were also belongs to the Kshatriyas class but due to the defeat in a battle with VAISTHA after which they became their subordinates. He raises many question against the political minded Hindus such as are you fit for political power even though you do not allow a class of your own countrymen like the untouchables to use public school, public well, public street, to wear what apparel or ornament they like, food they want to eat, he who emerged a revolutionary leader, approached the problem of Hindu caste system and the fate of suppressed human being from different perspective. In estimation of Dr. Ambedkar caste is a barrier to social progress and was the direct result of Hindu caste system.

According to him Varna and Caste were evil ideas. He was of the belief that by the eradication of the Varna system, a cohesive and egalitarian society may emerged the concept if equality and fraternity and viewed that every congressmen who was of the opinion that when one country is not fit to rule, another country must admit that one class is not fit to rule another class. If he talks about political reformation he criticized both Mahatma Gandhi as well as Congress Party. He said that Congress to be the sole representative of people of India including all communities'

But congress does not pay much emphasis on the interest of the untouchables and when he mentioned Gandhi, Ambedkar says that he give many quotes and sayings but no views and suggestions that were helpful for the development of un-trodden He was of the view that there should be reorganization and reconstruction of the society which relates to the abolition of caste system. High class Hindu never feel the necessity for agitating for the abolition of the caste system, rather they felt quite a greater urge to remove those evils such as child marriages, sati etc One important fact that deserves to be mentioned over here is that Gandhi could never rid his mind of a concept of Varna system and he never directly asked people to give up on caste system. On the other hand Dr. Ambedkar clearly mentioned outcaste is the byproduct of the caste system. There will be outcaste as long as there are castes. And nothing can emancipate the outcaste except the destruction of the caste system.

Political democracy cannot last unless there lies at the base of it social democracy. What does social democracy mean? It means a way of life which recognizes liberty, equality and fraternity as the principles of life.

-DR. BHIM RAO AMBEDKAR

Dr. Ambedkar's initiative for the abolition of caste system

Dr. B R Ambedkar throughout his lifetime was considered to be a controversial personality. He was a great nationalist who was less understood and more misunderstood by his own countrymen. But his worth could not be hidden for a long time, he began to be hailed by the people of the India as a great patriot throughout his life. There were various initiatives taken by him for the course of the memorandum that he submitted jointly with Roa Bahadur K. Srinivasan of the minority committee of the round table conference he had outlined the terms and conditions on which the depressed classes will consent to place themselves under a majority rule in a self governing India as follow:

- Equal citizenship and fundamental rights declaring the practice of untouchability as illegal.
- Free enjoyment of equal rights protected by adequate constitutional remedies.
- Protection against discrimination.
- Adequate representation to the depressed classes in the legislature. They must have the right to elect their representative by Universal Adult Suffrage.
- Adequate representation in the services.
- Redress against pre judicial action or neglect of interest and obligation should be imposed on the legislation and the executive to make adequate provision for the education, sanitation, recruitment and other matters of social and political advancement of the depressed classes.

Ambedkar was called upon to play a stupendous role in his capacity as chairman of the drafting committee of the constituent assembly and as a minister of Law in the Nehru Cabinet. He was entrusted with the responsibility of safeguarding the rights of every Indian, especially for depressed sections. A quick glance at the provisions enumerated in part III, IV and XVI of the Indian Constitution.

DR. B.R. AMBEDKAR AS A MASSIAH FOR DOWNTRODDEN

On his return to India in 1923, he founded, Bahishkrit Hitakarini Sabha with a main object of spreading education and improving the economic conditions of the oppressed classes. With a slogan of Educate-Agitate-Organized the social movement led by Dr. Ambedkar aimed at annihilation of the caste and the reconstruction of the Indian society on the basis of equality of human beings.

In 1927 he led the march at Mahad, Maharashtra to establish the rights of the untouchables to take water from the public Chawdar Lake. This marked the beginning of anti-caste and anti-priest movement. The temple entry movement launched by B.R. Ambedkar in 1930 at the Kalaram temple is another landmark in the struggle of human rights, political and social justice.

One of the greatest contributions of Dr. Ambedkar was in respect of fundamental rights and directive principles of state policy enshrined in the constitution of India. The fundamental rights provide for freedom, equality and abolition of untouchability and remedies to ensure the evolution of rights. The directive principles mentioned fair distribution of wealth and better living conditions for all.It was he, who forsook his high pedestal, lying down to their level, gives them a helping hand and raised them to human stature. For Indians, Ambedkar is no more a historical personality named Bhimrao Ramji Ambedkar. He is already metamorphosed into a symbol-a symbol for their collective aspiration and an icon for the thesis of their emancipation. Human history is replete with such icons; rather it is largely made of them.

In 16th century the word caste was derived from the Spanish and Portuguese word Casta, which means race or lineage. Caste system is an example of rigid social inequality from the perspective of social organization and system of values. So far as social organization of caste is concerned, there is division of society into groups ranking in a different hierarchy and in a system of values, caste provide legitimacy to the concept of social inequality among the masses as well as give importance to the idea of purity and pollution. The roots of Hindu caste system were already in place between 1000 and 1500 B.C. When the Aryans settled near the Indus river valley. The Rig Veda a sacred text from the period describe four main Varna in traditional Hindu society : Brahmanas ; the class of priests and teachers ; Kshatriyas, the warrior class who were the rulers and soldiers ; Vaishyas, the commercial class of artisans, traders and cultivators and Shudras; the servant and peasant class.

The word caste signifies breed, race and rank which came into use for the first time in 1563 A.D. by Gracia De Orta wrote - no one can changes from his father's trade and all those of the same caste of the shoe maker are the same. To Hindu, however, the concept of caste has a narrower and more precise meaning, referring to the smaller sub-groups defined by subtle distinction of birth, intermarriage and occupation. The four Varna's described in Rig Veda comprises more than 2000 sub castes .Beneath these caste is a fifth population group- those without any caste, literally, outcastes. They are treated as Untouchables. The Indian Constitution of 1950 made untouchability illegal. Today these people call themselves Dalits (oppressed) .

In India Caste System consists of two different concepts that is Varna and Jati, the real concept of Varna has almost disappeared in the present context and has changed into Jati. The former was based on color of the skin and later on birth.

It is the religious and social institution of Hindu peoples who comprised about 80% of India's population. The rest of India is Muslim, Christian, Sikh, Jain or Buddhist. Caste is such a deep rooted and pervasive concept, it is a rigid form of stratification system, in which mobility of rank and status is not allowed. However, that it has also influenced Muslims, Christians and Sikhs, for instance, they have separate churches for dalits and non dalits Christians. The 50 million Indians who live in tribal community predate the Aryan and Dravidian civilization. They are members of backward classes, they are not the part of Hindu society even then, they have started observing untouchability towards Dalits- who themselves have a caste hierarchy.

ORIGIN OF CASTE SYSTEM

Although, it is difficult to establish as to when the caste system originated, but there is no doubt that the institution of caste for the convenience of the ruling class leading to successful administration by them. There are different theories about the establishment of the caste system. These are Religious mystical, Biological, Socio-historical theories.

Religious Theory

The religious theory explained how the four Varna's were founded, but they do not explained how the Jaats in each Varna or the untouchables were founded. According to Rig Veda, the ancient Hindu book, the primal man- Purush - destroyed himself to create human society. The different Varnas were created from different part of his bodies. The Brahmans were created from his Head; the kshtriyas from his Hands; the Vaishyas from his Thighs and the Shudras from his Feet. Other religious theory claims that the Varna's were created from the body organs of Brahma, who is the creator of the world. According to Iravati Krave : the four rank system was creation of ruling class which originally had a three rank system in which whatever the differences of rank all people had right to certain rituals and sacraments from birth to death.

Biological theory

The biological theories claims that all existing things, animated and in animated, inherent three qualities in different apportionment. Sattva attributes includes wisdom, intelligence, honesty, goodness, and other positive qualities. Rajas attributes includes velour, passion, pride and other passionate qualities. Tamas attributes includes dullness, stupidity. Lack of creativity and other negative qualities. According to these attributes Brahmans inherent Sattva qualities. Kshatriyas and Vaishyas inherent Rajas qualities and Shudras inherent Tamas qualities.

In ancient India the religion had a prominent place; the king was considered the image of God. The Priest King accorded different position to different functional groups. According to Senart, like human beings food also inherent different dosage of these qualities but he explained the origin of caste system on the basis of prohibition regarding sacramental food. He holds that the followers of a particular deity considered themselves the descendants of the same ancestors and offered a particular kind of food as offering to their deity. Those who believed in the same deity considered themselves as different from those who believed in some other deity.

Socio historical theory

The socio historical theory explains the creation of the Varna, Jaats and untouchables. According to this theory the caste system begins with the arrival of Aryans in India. Before the Aryans there were other communities in India of other origins among them Negrito, Mongoloid, Austroloid and Dravidian. When the Aryans arrived in India their main contact was with the Dravidians and Austroloids. The Aryans disregarded the local culture, they begin conquering and taken control over regions in north India and at the same time pushed the local people towards the south, jungles and mountains in north India.The Aryans organized among themselves in three groups. The first was of a warrior called

Rajayana later they changed their name to kshatriya. The second group was of priest called Brahmans. The third group was of farmers and craftsmen and they were called as Vaishyas. In order to secure their status the Aryans resolved some social and religious rules which allowed only them to be the priest, warrior and the businessmen of the society. For instance: Maharashtra in West India, many think that the meaning of the name Maharashtra is great land but some claim that the name Maharashtra is derived from the Jaats called Mahar who were considered to be the original people of this region. In the caste hierarchy the dark-skinned Mahar were outcastes. The skin color was an important factor in the caste system.

The meaning of the word Varna is not class or status but skin color. In Hindu religious stories there were many wars between the good Aryans and a dark skinned demons and devils, but the real fact was that the dark skinned slaves were in fact the original residence of India, whom the Aryans coined as monsters, devils, demons and slaves.

Therefore the caste system did not come into existence all of a sudden or at a particular date. It is the result of the long process of social evolution. A number of factors played their part in the development of the present caste system enumerated as follows:

- Hereditary occupation.
- The desire of the Brahmans to keep themselves pure.
- The lack of rigid, unitary control of the state.
- The unwillingness of ruler to enforce a uniform standard of law and custom and their readiness to recognize the worrying custom of different groups as valid.
- Believe in re-incarnation and the doctrine of karma.
- Geographical isolation of the Indian peninsula.

- Static nature of Hindu society.
- Foreign invasion and rural social structure.

All these factors conspired to encourage the formation of small groups based on petty distinction from time to time. It may however be noted that the caste system is not specifically an institution of Hindus but it is a typical Indian institution. Further caste system is not a monopoly of India it existed and still exists in many parts of the world. What is unique in the Hindu caste system is that it alone classified some groups as untouchables and unapproachable.

ISSUES RELATING TO CASTE SYSTEM

According to P.N Bose,- the caste system has acted essentially to impose that attitude of money, needed to raise men from savagery but to stop them halfway on progress.

Disintegrating factor

The caste system has literally split up the society into hundreds of hereditary caste and sub castes and encouraged a spirit of exclusiveness and class-pride, narrowed the outlook and created wide gulfs between the various sections of the community. The caste system resulted in lots of evils because of its rigid rules. It perpetuates exploitation of the economically weaker and socially inferior caste. It protects the privileged caste and thus, builds up economic discontent and social prejudices. A person born in one caste was doomed to remain in it forever, and keep check on economic and intellectual advancement and a great stumbling block in way of social reforms, because it keeps economic and intellectual opportunities confined to a certain section of the population only and denies them to other. The Shudras and untouchables had to perform all the menial tasks. They could not do anything for their own development. The worst thing is that they cannot be permitted to devote himself to any educational or scientific profession, even when they have natural aptitudes and physical and intellectual equipment for it. Worthy and capable person are prevented by caste rigors from getting their proper and rightful places, even there next generation has to follow the same rigidness of caste system, and they too remain closed slaves and bonded labors. The caste system however is guilty of just the opposite demerit. It does not make proper provision for low-born talents or high-born incompetence.

Barred to religious ties;

As far as religion is concerned the lower caste people were not even allowed to touch the holy book and sacred literatures and they were devoid to enter into the temple. This problem has given scope for religious conversion. The lower caste people were getting converted into Islam and Christianity, due to the tyranny of upper caste. Along with these issues the old Hindu Law Marriage Act 1955 promotes Anuloma marriage i.e. a boy from upper caste can marry a girl from lower caste and prohibits Pratiloma marriage i.e. a girl from lower caste cannot marry a boy from upper caste. It also inflicted untold hardships on women through its insistence on practices like child marriages, prohibition of widow remarriage, seclusion of women etc. these have made the life of women miserable.History bears testimony that the issue of caste system sanctioned privileges to a section of society who understood themselves as a superior class and at the same time it inflicted a series of disabilities on their sections which continues from generation to generation.

Contrary to Democracy

Democracy is based on principle of equality, fraternity and liberty. On the other hand the caste system is based on inequality of status and opportunities, which often creates conflict and tension in the society. It acts as an obstacle in the normal and smooth functioning of democracy. No doubt India has got political freedom but it must be the concerned of every individual that real freedom cannot be cherished without attainment of the social and the economic democracy. It is unfortunate that the Indian society is sharply divided into various caste and sub caste which acts as a barrier due to rigidity and division of the society based on caste consideration.

Perpetuates Untouchability

The caste system has condemned large groups of people to a life of degradation without any hope of redemption. It has created Untouchables, an evil that has been sapping the very vitals of the society. This untouchability is reduced to the state of natural slavery and hindered the growth of brotherhood; hold off the national unity as it disallowed any type of social intercourse. B.R Ambedkar rightly said, Untouchability of Hindus is a rare phenomenon, humanity is any other part of the earth has never experienced it. There is no such thing in any other society. Really, the tyranny is perpetuated in the name of untouchabilty are the black lesson in human culture. . According to Mahatma Gandhi, untouchability is the hate fullest expression of caste.

Hindrance in the way of Modernization

The caste system obstructs the process of Modernization as it also restricts the mental development of an individual. Modern Indian intellect is, therefore burdened with the sense of contrition over the matter. Passions overwhelmingly carry us to a position of hostility towards any compromise, and the entire caste structure placed in the docks. Despite this it cannot be said that the caste system offers a place in which any group religion or occupation can fit in as a cooperating part of the society.

BHIM RAO AMBEDKARS: VISION

Bhim Rao Ambedkar was born in December 1981 in a Mahar community, an untouchable caste of Maharashtra. His father Ramji and grandfather Maloji was in military services. He was the youngest child of his parents and was just only five when his mother died. Thereafter his aunt took care of him. He was enrolled in a local school of Satara where he had to sit on the floor and his teacher would not touch his books as because he was untouchable. Facing so many hardships in his life B R Ambedkar continued his studies and passed his matriculation. In 1913 Maharaj OF Baroda awarded scholarship to B R Ambedkar and send him to America for attaining the degree of Masters, it was for the first time in his life he was not degraded for being Mahar.

He submerged himself in the studies and obtained the Degree of M.A, PHD from the University of Columbia. There after he proceeded to London but soon Baroda government ended his scholarship and bring him back. The Maharaja of Baroda appointed him as a Secretary but here also he faced discrimination because of being Mahar. In 1917 he returned to Bombay and joined syndrome college, Bombay as a professor of political economy on a temporary basis. the social treatment of other professors were so pathetic as they all belongs to high caste even they objected that Ambedkar can't drink water from the pot reserved for the professional staff. When he started legal practice in the High Court of Judicature, Bombay. He had no money even to obtain sanad. He had joint the appellate side of the bar. The solicitor would not condensed to have any business dealing with him because of untouchability .therefore, all these circumstances forced him to be a great rebel against the Hindu orthodoxy and its discriminatory treatment to turns his mind for searching a cult where a man is not discriminated by the another man.

Dr. Ambedkar played a significant role for the upliftment of downtrodden. He was considered as messiah for suppressed class as he belongs to untouchable's community. He experienced caste discrimination right from the childhood, that's why he raises the issues related to untouchability there are many leaders who raise their voice for the down trodden of India, but the most significant, eminent actions were taken by B R Ambedkar because he himself faced such problems ,After noticing the evils of prevailing caste system and its impacts on suppressed human being prompted founding father of the Constitution of India to create an egalitarian society wherein justice, social, economic and political right prevails which includes equality of status and opportunity may be available to everyone irrespective of caste system.

No doubt India has got political freedom and has political democracy, but it must be the concerned of everyone that real freedom cannot be cherished without attainment of social and economic democracy. It is unfortunate that the Indian society is sharply divided into various caste and sub caste which is obstacle due to rigidity segregation and division of the society based on rigid caste consideration. B R Ambedkar was impressed enough by the conduct and humanism of the great social reformers like Budhha, Kabir and Jyotiba Phule. He declared that Untouchables must leave the Hindu culture and accept another religion instead, and he himself embraced Buddhism.

Dr. Ambedkar criticized old Law books like Manusmriti and Arthshastras who showed the inferiority and bitterness towards the suppressed class. He also criticized the higher standard of Brahmans who are category above of all. The Brahmans are somehow responsible for social exploitation and the backwardness of untouchables.

Ambedkar also rejected that there were no such invasion of Aryans as mentioned in the ancient Vedic and Sanskrit literature. He argued that Shudras were not dark skinned but Shudras were also belongs to the Kshatriyas class but due to the defeat in a battle with VAISTHA after which they became their subordinates. He raises many question against the political minded Hindus such as are you fit for political power even though you do not allow a class of your own countrymen like the untouchables to use public school, public well, public street, to wear what apparel or ornament they like, food they want to eat, he who emerged a revolutionary leader, approached the problem of Hindu caste system and the fate of suppressed human being from different perspective. In estimation of Dr. Ambedkar caste is a barrier to social progress and was the direct result of Hindu caste system.

According to him Varna and Caste were evil ideas. He was of the belief that by the eradication of the Varna system, a cohesive and egalitarian society may emerged the concept if equality and fraternity and viewed that every congressmen who was of the opinion that when one country is not fit to rule, another country must admit that one class is not fit to rule another class. If he talks about political reformation he criticized both Mahatma Gandhi as well as Congress Party. He said that Congress to be the sole representative of people of India including all communities'

But congress does not pay much emphasis on the interest of the untouchables and when he mentioned Gandhi, Ambedkar says that he give many quotes and sayings but no views and suggestions that were helpful for the development of un-trodden He was of the view that there should be reorganization and reconstruction of the society which relates to the abolition of caste system. High class Hindu never feel the necessity for agitating for the abolition of the caste system, rather they felt quite a greater urge to remove those evils such as child marriages, sati etc One important fact that deserves to be mentioned over here is that Gandhi could never rid his mind of a concept of Varna system and he never directly asked people to give up on caste system. On the other hand Dr. Ambedkar clearly mentioned outcaste is the byproduct of the caste system. There will be outcaste as long as there are castes. And nothing can emancipate the outcaste except the destruction of the caste system.

Political democracy cannot last unless there lies at the base of it social democracy. What does social democracy mean? It means a way of life which recognizes liberty, equality and fraternity as the principles of life.-**DR. BHIM RAO AMBEDKAR**

Dr. Ambedkar's initiative for the abolition of caste system

Dr. B R Ambedkar throughout his lifetime was considered to be a controversial personality. He was a great nationalist who was less understood and more misunderstood by his own countrymen. But his worth could not be hidden for a long time, he began to be hailed by the people of the India as a great patriot throughout his life. There were various initiatives taken by him for the course of the memorandum that he submitted jointly with Roa Bahadur K. Srinivasan of the minority committee of the round table conference he had outlined the terms and conditions on which the depressed classes will consent to place themselves under a majority rule in a self governing India as follow:

- Equal citizenship and fundamental rights declaring the practice of untouchability as illegal.
- Free enjoyment of equal rights protected by adequate constitutional remedies.
- Protection against discrimination.
- Adequate representation to the depressed classes in the legislature. They must have the right to elect their representative by Universal Adult Suffrage.
- Adequate representation in the services.
- Redress against pre judicial action or neglect of interest and obligation should be imposed on the legislation and the executive to make adequate provision for the education, sanitation, recruitment and other matters of social and political advancement of the depressed classes.

Ambedkar was called upon to play a stupendous role in his capacity as chairman of the drafting committee of the constituent assembly and as a minister of Law in the Nehru Cabinet. He was entrusted with the responsibility of safeguarding the rights of every Indian, especially for depressed sections. A quick glance at the provisions enumerated in part III, IV and XVI of the Indian Constitution.

CONTRIBUTION TO THE DEVELOPMENTS OF THE DALITS IN INDIA

Indian society is made of different castes, sub castes and religions. We may underline classification of the society into four Varnas like Brahmins, Kshatriyas, Vaishyas and Shudras. Mukundrao Patil writes "India is a strange place, which collects all sorts of social groups, divided by different religions, thoughts, practices and understandings". This division of caste took people from Brahmin community on the top considering them leaders of education and „Shudras were pulled at the bottom. They were looked at as the slaves by other three Varnas. Due to this they had to suffer from social, economical, political, physical and psychological exploitation. Disliking such pathetic condition of Shudras Abedkar came to the front to fight for the upliftment and enhancement of Shudras. He fought for equality and basic rights to them. The two basic acts named Chaudar Movement and opening the doors of Hindu temples to the Harijans for showing them a path that all human beings are equal.

Dr. Babasaheb Ambedkar also had to face lot of challenges at the different stages of life and during education. His birth in untouchable family did not cease to bring him in the pond which is full of humiliation and insults. He was not permitted to satisfy his thrust by drinking water in the school. He was made to feel differentiated from other students by sitting in the far away corner of the school by the teachers. Due to spirit of intelligence Babasheb was successful in achieving degrees in different fields like M. A. in Ancient Indian Commerce, Ph. D., M. Sc. in Economics D.sc in Economics and Bar-at-law. Surprised by Ambedkar s scholarship Prof. Seligman Wrote „He is an excellent student and a nice fellow, moderate, broad and able, and I know that you will be glad to be of service to him in the prosecution of his researches. Knowing the fact that "Experience is the best teacher, Dr. Babasaheb Ambedkar worked at various places in various positions. He worked as Military secretary to the Maharaja Sayajirao Gaikwad and professor of political Economy in Bombay. U.S.A. and Great Britain are the two places where Babasaheb could make his career. Ambedkar s powerful thoughts did not allow him to sit silent and let the Shudras suffer at the hands of Savarnas. Sparing lot of his life time to the common people, he really gave voice to the untouchables to struggle in the life. Babasaheb Ambedkar "played three roles: that of a caste leader, that of an untouchable spokesman, and that of a national statesman") He criticized caste-ridden Hindu society and Hindu social structure through his writings and spoke on India s development. Ambedkar s role in framing the Indian constitution was catalytic.

Ambedkar s Views on Democratic Society are very much valuable from the point of democratic structure of the society in India. Realizing a very dangerous situation of untouchables in the country Dr. Babasaheb Ambedkar firmly decided to spare his life time to develop socio-economic condition of this section of the society. To him freedom of the people was the great need for it and no freedom of the nation. Freedom of the people is freedom of the country. If the citizens are not allowed to open their lips freely to express their feelings the concept of the free nation fails. When the process of exchanging thoughts stops the progress of the people and the country seems to be stopped. No one caste or religion is better or greater than the other. Their ways of life and doctrines are the same. He said political democracy must have roots in social democracy. He profoundly declared that the democratic form of the society should have base for democratic form of government. It is obligatory on the part of democratic society to have attitude of mind, respect and equality among the people. According to Ambedkar democratic society must be free from stiff social impediments. Focusing on social democracy Ambedkar said it is a way of life which gives primary preferences to liberty, equality and fraternity. They are the principles of life.The efforts were taken by the Indian saints and social workers to make free the Dalits from the imposed powers of upper classes. But they did it on the philosophical and religious level and rejected political base.They also strongly supported Varna system in Indian society. Ambedkar is called as a social Rebel because he dared to express his views against exploitation of the Dalits and he took efforts to stop the exploitation at various levels. Ambedkar fought against the thought that the present position of person has been decided by the good and bad deeds of his past life. He also revolted against exploitation of the downtrodden and inequality. He undertook a task of inspiring the untouchables to raise voice against the Hindu Social system. With gallant efforts Ambedkar was successful in ceasing the slavery of the Dalit community.

Revolutionary decision on Chowdar Tank by Dr. Babasaheb Ambedkar is one of the golden events in the life of the down trodden people. The untouchables were not allowed to use water from public watering places, wells, schools, colleges, and hospitals which is the basic right of all human race of using natural sources. The small stream of water or river do not discriminate human being on the basis of caste, religion, gender or colour whenever he or she goes to them to fulfill thirst. Hence, The Bombay Legislative Assembly passed resolution on this issue which was brought by the staunch social reformer Mr. S.K. Bole in 1923. The untouchables were not allowed to take water from the Chowdar tank in Mahad also. The Hindus were the major obstacles. This event becomes the root cause of inspiration to Dr. Ambedkar to begin agitation against the prevention of using water from the tank. Taking the progressive step the Municipality of Mahad made declaration of opening the Chowdar tank to the untouchables. This revolutionary decision in 1924 gave justice to the downtrodden community on using natural sources of water and them to fill happy all over the country. In the leadership of Ambedkar ten thousand volunteers on 19th March 1927 came together to begin peaceful March for their right of drinking water from the Municipal tank.

Conference against the „Manuscript at Mahad helped to whisper the thoughts of awareness in the minds of the untouchables. The first conference took place at Mahad on 25 December 1927, which was attended by thousands of Satyagrahis. Removing the obstacles created by the Hindus the conference started at the evening with Ambedkar s addressing speech. Many resolutions regarding socio-political and religious upliftment of the untouchables were passed on. „*The Manusmriti*' was poured in the ears of the untouchables if they listened or red the Vedas. Therefore, in the conference, they passed resolution against „*The Manusmriti*' by burning a copy of it. Buring the old Manusmriti Ambedkar gave voice to have a new one. The purpose behind this work was to bring in action the Hindu code which governs the life of people in great majority.Everybody before the God is the same. The untouchables were not allowed in the Hindu temples. The thought „like others we are human beings did not permit him sound sleep. Using method of „Satyagraha Ambedkar organized the untouchables for opening the doors of the Hindu temples. Consequently, the Satyagrahas like Amravati Satyagraha in 1927, Parvati Satyagraha in 1929-30, and Satyagraha of Nasik for temple entry took place. Ambedkar continuously used Gandhi s principles of Ahimsa and Satyagraha for gaining social and religious rights to untouchables.

Ambedkar wanted to reproduce atmosphere of equality in the untouchable community and awareness in them that all human beings are equal. Nobody is small, or big and pure or impure on the basis of birth in the caste. All are the children of God. According to him social upliftment of the down trodden is the only solution for this cause. He advised people to give up old customs and traditions and lead clean life. The art of speech gave Ambedkar a chance of becoming member of the Bombay Legislative Council from 1926 to 1934. It leaded him to support the Bills of elevation of untouchables from socio-economic point of view.In order to get share of the untouchables in the politics Ambedkar stood in the front row for signing the Poona Pact. It gave opportunity to the untouchables to establish their identity in the politics also. Because of this act some seats are kept reserve for the downtrodden community in the Hindu constituencies. Taking into consideration of Ambedkar s work for the upliftment of untouchable and his remarkable services to the nation the government of India awarded him „Bharat Ratna in 1990.

Mahatma Jyotiba Phule gave more life time for working on education, social and political progress of the lower community. It was carried out by Babasaheb Ambedkar. Thus Ambedkar s contribution in socio-political and economics upliftment of the untouchables is ever important. Acquiring sound knowledge in the subjects like economics and law he fought for socio-economic and political equality of his community. Babbasaheb Ambedkar used politics as a weapon to get an equal status in the Indian politics. Thus, Dr. Babasaheb Ambedkar focused on three principles Justice, Equality and Fraternity. His devotion for the frame work of Indian constitution reflects his dedicated, outstanding and studious nature.

POLITICAL IMPLICATION

Chapter 4

THE SCHEDULED CASTE'S FEDERATION AND CASTE POLITICS

Ambedkar founded the SCF in July, 1942 in order to signal, as the name of the organization suggests, a shift in the political strategy: the emphasis was again on caste. The immediate reason for this decision was the Cripps Mission formula, which was submitted in March 1942 to resolve India's constitutional impasse. It proposed the election of a Constituent Assembly without taking into account any of the demands of Untouchables, whereas Muslims were virtually guaranteed the prospect of a separate state, Pakistan. Ambedkar was not prepared to see his community's interests sacrificed in this manner: Hit is quite obvious that the proposal for a Constituent Assembly is intended to win over the Congress, while the proposal for Pakistan is designed to win over the Muslim League. How do the proposals deal with the Depressed Classes? To put it shortly, they are bound hand and foot and handed over to the caste Hindus. They offer them nothing: stone instead of bread. For the Constituent Assembly is nothing but a betrayal of the Depressed Classes ... If they are there, they cannot have a free, independent decisive vote. In the first place, the representative of the Depressed Classes will be in a hopeless minority. In the second place, all decisions of the Constituent Assembly are not required by a unanimous vote".

In reaction to Cripps's proposal the All India Depressed Classes' Conference met at Nagpur. It brought together 70,000 delegates from Punjab, the United Provinces, Bengal and Madras Presidency, but in even larger numbers from Bombay Presidency, the Central Provinces and Berar. The first resolution voted on this occasion demanded a separate electorate for Untouchables; the second sought the establishment of separate villages for Untouchables, 'at a distance from the Hindu villages'; and the third announced the creation of the Scheduled Castes' Federation . The creation of the SCF therefore reflected a new mood~ a new sense of identity among Untouchables. The Scheduled Castes wished to be recognized as a minority in the same way as Muslims were, and, as a consequence, sought the benefit, not only of separate electorate, but also of separate territories. From] 926 onwards Ambedkar had suggested that Untouchables should settle new lands; and in 1929, he had even proposed surveying unoccupied but cultivable areas of Sind and of Indore state, whose Maharajah he was close to .The general guidelines set out in the Nagpur resolutions were clarified by the Executive Committee of the SCF in September 1944, meeting in Madras. One motion reiterated that 'the Scheduled Castes are a distinct and separate element in the national life of India and that they are religious minority in a sense far more real than the Sikhs and Muslims can be and within the meaning of the Cripps Proposals'. Another resolution stipulated that no Constitution would be deemed acceptable to the Scheduled Castes if it did not have their consent. This proposition was conditional on the fulfillment of several demands: a separate electorate, a guarantee of representation within the executive and a special form of taxation for their own villages.The notion of Dalit villages crystallized around the same time.

Ambedkar rightly attributes the decline of the Justice Party to a fonn of careerism which led it to betray its natural constituency. This critique was in tune with Ambedkar's reorientation towards a greater focus on Untouchables per se, a project of which the SCF was the spearhead. As he declared in Madras: "You should realize what our object is ... It is not fighting for a few jobs or a few conveniences. It is the highest cause that we have ever cherished in our hearts. That is to see that we are recognized as the Governing community".64 During a meeting organized by the Railway Employees' Union in Madras, he declared in the same vein, according to some press reports, that: 'without minimizing the importance o~ Trade Union, he would like to emphasize the importance of capturing political power'.

The elections of 1945-46 were to reveal that the party stilI had a long way to go before achieving such ends. They had a dual purpose in that they were about renewing the provincial assemblies and endowing India with a Constituent Assembly. The SCF fared badly in both respects, gaining only two seats in the provincial assemblies, one in Bengal, the other in the Central Provinces and Berar. This setback partly reflected the voting system. In the primaries in which only Untouchables voted, the SCF gained more votes than the Congress in the Presidencies of Madras and Bombay and in the Central Provinces. But these good results could not translate into a commensurate number of seats because of the electoral system. The situation in the United Provinces was especially revealing of the distortions inherent in the electoral system. There twenty seats were reserved for the Scheduled Castes, including four urban constituencies, which were the only ones the SCF contested. In the primaries, nine of the party's candidates were successful as against four for Congress - but in the second round the latter won all the seats due to the support of non-Dalit voters. The most dramatic result occurred in Agra, where four SCF candidates polled 46.39 percent of valid votes as against to 27.1 percent for four Congress candidates.

This state of affairs could only strengthen Ambedkar's stance in favor of a separate electorate for the Untouchables. His only hope in this regard lay with the British. He went to England in late 1946 to present his views in this regard. In spite of pressing his demands, Ambedkar was not heard by the British, who considered that the failure of the SCF in the elections of 1945- 6 did not endow it with the status of an important player, or even merit a particular role in the Constituent Assembly.

In addition to the impact made by the electoral system, a much plausible explanation of the SCF's defeat lay in the tiny number of candidates nominated by the party: it did not field any at all in 129 of the 151 seats reserved for Untouchables, reflecting its organizational weakness. As Bandyopadhyay tartly pointed out: "the Federation had no organizational machinery".68 In fact, the general opinion of the scholars on Federation suggests that it had no network of party branches and only a handful of cadres. The party relied very heavily on Ambedkar who was unable to spend much time in campaigning given his other commitments as a member of the Viceroy's government. Zelliot underlines that he was also preoccupied in writing *What Congress and Gandhi have done to Untouchables,69* one more indication that he was unquestionably as much an intellectual as a politician - if not as much an organization man.

As party leader Ambedkar oscillated between two strategies. He tried first to attract not only Dalits but all kinds of workers by establishing the ILP. But the broad agenda of this party was hard to reconcile with the core Dalit ideology and sociology of Ambedkarism.77 Hence the launch of the SCF was an effort to hark back to the cause of the Untouchables. However, the scope of the party turned out to be too limited and therefore Ambedkar went back to the initial philosophy of the ILP in a different way: with the RPI he tried to set up an organization representing all those of low status, the Scheduled Castes, the Other Backward Classes and the Scheduled Tribes. The class option, as is underlined by J. Gokhale, was based on a reading of Untouchability in socio-economic terms which allows Untouchables to seek allies among other castes suffering from similar handicaps. Thus it can be witnessed that Ambedkar was not only a social reformer with a philosophical bent of mind but was also a remarkable statesman searching for an electoral strategy and changing his positions as per the demands of electoral politics.

But, in Ambedkar, these components of electoral politics worked only as the indispensable means to serve the greater end of social emancipation through the agency of politics.

Reorganization of States

Indian state has ever since colonial era faced with the problems of linguistic reorganization of states. Partition of Bengal in 1905-6 was probably the first political issue to have caused the first mass mobilization on Indian subcontinent. This was followed by a series of linguistic agitations to be culminated in 1950s when Indian. government was forced to appoint State Reorganization Commission (SRC) to study the issue of reorganization of States along linguistic lines. The Congress Party remained oscillating regarding this issue. At the Nagpur session in 1920, the Party under the leadership of Gandhi adopted the linguistic redistribution of provinces as a clear political objective and in the following year the Congress was reorganized along these lines. In 1927 the Congress adopted a resolution that "the time has come for the redistribution of provinces on a linguistic basis" and constituting Andhra, Utkal, Sind and Karnataka into separate provinces could make a beginning. Members supporting the resolution referred to the right of self-determination of the people speaking the same language, and bound by the same tradition and culture. However, the partition of the country and the riots immediately following it brought a change in the thinking of Congress leaders.

In the Constituent Assembly, on 27 November 1947, soon after partition, Prime Minister Nehru argued, "First things must come first, and the first thing is the security and stability of India". This change is also reflected in the reports of the Dar Commission and the JVP Commission, which showed that the reconstitution of provinces solely on linguistic basis was no longer taken for granted.[78] Between 1951 and 1953 the agitation for the formation of a separate state of Andhra became acute, and its formation in 1953 led to strident demands by people in other regions. There were demands for a Greater Gujarat, Maha Punjab, United Maharashtra,

Maha Vidharbha, and a separate Karnataka etc., many of which conflicted with each other. In the backdrop of this, SRC was appointed and asked to submit its report. Discussing the seminal issue of linguistic reorganization the SRC initially pointed out its advantages. It was of the view that in a federal system each unit must be homogenous and in India, "language provides the only rational basis of for reconstructing the states, for it reflects the social and cultural pattern of living obtaining in well-defined regions of the country".79 Each state could use its own language for purposes of administration and education. This would encourage the people' s participation in decision- making and welfare programmes, and all linguistic groups would gain "political and economic justice". In contrast, in multilingual states, all the benefits of government policies would go to the majority community, creating animosities. The Commission argued that unilingual rather than composite states would be better, particularly as many states were already unilingual, and such a promise had already been made during the national movement.

At the same time, the SRC also emphasized the dangers inherent in unilingual states and suggested means to overcome them. Unilingual states could encourage excJusivism and weaken the unity of the nation, which was already fragile. The use of regional languages would mean lack of common language of administration and common educational standard. Even national planning would be vulnerable and maximum utilization of resources would not be possible leading to uneven economic development. The Commission also warned against the consequences of the notion of a 'homeland' for each language group, and overemphasis on state autonomy, which could lead to regional loyalties. Finally, the SRC recommended that the linguistic factor should not be deciding but the other factors, such as financial viability, size, etc., should also be considered, and each case separately considered on its own merit. When the evidence had been examined. the Commission recommended a redrawing of India's political geography along lines, which more or less coincided, with many of the linguistically based demands.

On the basis of these factors, the Commission recommended the break-up of the three categories of states (A, B and C) and the creation of only two types, namely, states and union territories, the latter being centrally governed. While part A states provided the standard and were to be maintained with some changes, the other two categories would be integrated into the nearby part A states on the basis of language.

Sixteen states on the basis of language were to be formed, with the exception of the bilingual states of Bombay and Punjab, and all remaining minorities in them, linguistic or otherwise, were to be granted safeguards within the Constitution. The interval between the submission of the SRC's report in December 1955 and the official demarcation of states on 1 November 1956, was marked by demands and counter-demands by various groups based upon the linguistic principle, which forced the government to modify some recommendations of the Commission. Thus the reorganization of the states as it was carried out in 1956 was in response to the strident and often violent and popular pressures of the time. Members of the Congress party in the states, particularly Maharashtra, Karnataka and Andhra, also were insistent and made representations before the SRC for linguistic reconstitution. Many and varied groups competed for recognition as units of the newly designed Union. While some felt that Nehru had bowed to pressures, others believed that he had bowed to democracy. which more or less coincided, with many of the linguistically based demands. On the basis of these factors, the Commission recommended the break-up of the three categories of states (A, B and C) and the creation of only two types, namely, states and union territories, the latter being centrally governed. While part A states provided the standard and were to be maintained with some changes, the other two categories would be integrated into the nearby part A states on the basis of language.

Sixteen states on the basis of language were to be formed, with the exception of the bilingual states of Bombay and Punjab, and all remaining minorities in them, linguistic or otherwise, were to be granted safeguards within the Constitution. The interval between the submission of the SRC's report in December 1955 and the official demarcation of states on 1 November 1956, was marked by demands and counter-demands by various groups based upon the linguistic principle, which forced the government to modify some recommendations of the Commission. Thus the reorganization of the states as it was carried out in 1956 was in response to the strident and often violent and popular pressures of the time. Members of the Congress party in the states, particularly Maharashtra, Karnataka and Andhra, also were insistent and made representations before the SRC for linguistic reconstitution. Many and varied groups competed for recognition as units of the newly designed Union. While some felt that Nehru had bowed to pressures, others believed that he had bowed to democracy. which more or less coincided, with many of the linguistically based demands. On the basis of these factors, the Commission recommended the break-up of the three categories of states (A, B and C) and the creation of only two types, namely, states and union territories, the latter being centrally governed. While part A states provided the standard and were to be maintained with some changes, the other two categories would be integrated into the nearby part A states on the basis of language.

Sixteen states on the basis of language were to be formed, with the exception of the bilingual states of Bombay and Punjab, and all remaining minorities in them, linguistic or otherwise, were to be granted safeguards within the Constitution. The interval between the submission of the SRC's report in December 1955 and the official demarcation of states on 1 November 1956, was marked by demands and counter-demands by various groups based upon the linguistic principle, which forced the government to modify some recommendations of the Commission. Thus the reorganization of the states as it was carried out in 1956 was in response to the strident and often violent and popular pressures of the time. Members of the Congress party in the states, particularly Maharashtra, Karnataka and Andhra, also were insistent and made representations before the SRC for linguistic reconstitution. Many and varied groups competed for recognition as units of the newly designed Union. While some felt that Nehru had bowed to pressures, others believed that he had bowed to democracy. which more or less coincided, with many of the linguistically based demands. On the basis of these factors, the Commission recommended the break-up of the three categories of states (A, B and C) and the creation of only two types, namely, states and union territories, the latter being centrally governed. While part A states provided the standard and were to be maintained with some changes, the other two categories would be integrated into the nearby part A states on the basis of language.

Sixteen states on the basis of language were to be formed, with the exception of the bilingual states of Bombay and Punjab, and all remaining minorities in them, linguistic or otherwise, were to be granted safeguards within the Constitution. The interval between the submission of the SRC's report in December 1955 and the official demarcation of states on 1 November 1956, was marked by demands and counter-demands by various groups based upon the linguistic principle, which forced the government to modify some recommendations of the Commission. Thus the reorganization of the states as it was carried out in 1956 was in response to the strident and often violent and popular pressures of the time. Members of the Congress party in the states, particularly Maharashtra, Karnataka and Andhra, also were insistent and made representations before the SRC for linguistic reconstitution. Many and varied groups competed for recognition as units of the newly designed Union. While some felt that Nehru had bowed to pressures, others believed that he had bowed to democracy. which more or less coincided, with many of the linguistically based demands. On the basis of these factors, the Commission recommended the break-up of the three categories of states (A, B and C) and the creation of only two types, namely, states and union territories, the latter being centrally governed. While part A states provided the standard and were to be maintained with some changes, the other two categories would be integrated into the nearby part A states on the basis of language.

Sixteen states on the basis of language were to be formed, with the exception of the bilingual states of Bombay and Punjab, and all remaining minorities in them, linguistic or otherwise, were to be granted safeguards within the Constitution. The interval between the submission of the SRC's report in December 1955 and the official demarcation of states on 1 November 1956, was marked by demands and counter-demands by various groups based upon the linguistic principle, which forced the government to modify some recommendations of the Commission. Thus the reorganization of the states as it was carried out in 1956 was in response to the strident and often violent and popular pressures of the time. Members of the Congress party in the states, particularly Maharashtra, Karnataka and Andhra, also were insistent and made representations before the SRC for linguistic reconstitution. Many and varied groups competed for recognition as units of the newly designed Union. While some felt that Nehru had bowed to pressures, others believed that he had bowed to democracy.

INCOMPATIBILITY OF PARLIAMENTARY DEMOCRACY WITH STATE-SOCIALISM

On more than one occasion Ambedkar pointed out the limitation of parliamentary democracy in ensuring economic equality to the masses. Ambedkar believed that there was a close connection between individual liberty and the form of the economic structure of society. In September 1943, posing the question why Parliamentary Democracy had failed to benefit the poor, the laboring and downtrodden classes in ensuring them liberty, property and pursuit of happiness, he identified two main causes which were either related to wrong ideology or wrong organization or both.3o As regards ideology, he stated that what ruined Parliamentary Democracy was the idea of *'freedom of contract'*.

The idea became sanctified and was upheld in the name of liberty. Parliamentary Democracy took no notice of economic inequalities and did not care to examine the result of 'freedom of contract' on the parties to the contract should they be unequal. It did not mind if 'freedom of contract' gave the strong opportunity to defraud the weak. The result was that parliamentary democracy, in starting out as a protagonist of liberty, has continuously added to the economic wrongs of the poor, the downtrodden and disinherited. Ambedkar, therefore, argued for a change in the very framework of 'freedom of contract'. He suggested state ownership *in* agriculture, basic and key industries and national insurance and their organization in a way that would lead to the highest productivity and at the same time promote fair distribution of income.

The implementation of state-socialism was not, however, to be left to parliamentary democracy, that is, to the legislature to bring it into being by the ordinary process of law.Ambedkar argued that one essential condition for the success of the *planned economy* was that it must not be liable to suspension or abandonment; it must be permanent. Such pennanence could not be given in a parliamentary democracy since the government would keep changing. The economic structure of the society to be modeled on state-socialism could not, therefore, be left to the exigencies of ordinary laws with a simple majority whose political future was never detennined by the national cause. Political democracy was, therefore, unsuited for this purpose, which could be better served by 'state-socialism' by the law of the constitution, so that it remained beyond the reach of parliamentary majority to suspend, amend or abrogate it. Such constitutional enactment would enable the retention of both socialism and parliamentary democracy.

Thus it can easily be seen that Ambedkar remains unhesitant in ruling out any parliamentary democracy unless it is backed by pennanent state-socialism and in Indian case he suggested that the programs for the poor and downtrodden classes of Indian society should be made central to the planning process. Ambedkar argued for industrialization as 'the surest means to rescue the people from poverty' .

Individual-cum-Society Friendly State

Ambedkar regards human rights as natural and inherent in the individual and holds that "the individual has certain inalienable rights". He builds his theory of social and political organization around his central concept of the individual and his rights. He speaks of state as based on a comprehensive social principle. The state exists not only to prevent injustice, tyranny and oppression but also to create such social and economic conditions that all men may be happy. In Ambedkar's view, the individual, not the state, is the object of supreme value and the state is a human organization to promote the individual's good. Ambedkar maintains that no government should violate the fundamental rights of man. For, some rights are so essential that no human society can be prosperous without them. From humanistic viewpoint, he is opposed to all kinds of discrimination in administration, even in private factories and commercial concerns, on the grounds of race, creed, and social status. He believes that society can do nothing without some organized power. He again insists that some kind of government is essential for maintaining peace and prosperity among men, particularly, when people fail to abide by law and order. Such is, to him, the mission of a good government. And in fact, without such quality, a true democratic society can not be established.

Similarly Ambedkar wants a good, moral government, to protect the rights of the people in all their legitimate functions. As regards the *'Fonns ofGovemment'*, Ambedkar favors *Democracy,* for he says "in anarchy and dictatorship, liberty is lost".34 He realized that dictatorship and anarchy are both incompatible with individual's liberty. For this reason, he feels the need of a sufficiently strong government under which the liberty would be well protected, and yet certain functional and Constitutional checks should be brought to bear upon the government so that the individual's liberty is not jeopardized.The solidarity and unity of society, according to Ambedkar, consists of 'the social need for protecting the best, having common rules of morality, and safeguarding the growth of the individual' .35 How far it becomes an actual state of society depends upon the efficient and proper functioning of government. He accords recognition to the democratic principle of rule by the majority (but not communal majority), while being conscious of the fact that the majority-rule may not necessarily be in the interest of the whole of the community, and on the contrary, may result into oppression of the individual or minorities. His main concern, therefore, is to safeguard the individual as against the tyranny of the majority. And this he aims to achieve not by taking away all power from the Government and reducing it to a nullity; but by formulating a scheme of 'checks and balances' on the lines of the American Constitution. Looked at from the above viewpoint, Ambedkar maintains that the will of the majority is essential for good governments, but it should necessarily provide concessions and considerations to the will of the minorities.

Linguistic Nationalism in Ambedkar

Ambedkar, after a realistic analysis of the problem of linguism and its implications, arrived at some definite conclusions concerning the structure and organization of states, the component units of the Indian federation. Ambedkar fmnly believes that in general, 'one state, one language' is a universal feature of almost every state - Germany, France, Italy, England, U.S.A etc., in the Western hemisphere. It is a general 'rule' and not a 'dogma' wherever there has been a departure from this rule; there has been a danger to the state. The danger of disintegration and degeneration is inherent in multilingual states. He says that

India cannot escape this fate if it continues to be a congery of mixed states. A multilingual state is thus unstable and a unilingual state is stable.A state, Ambedkar says, is built on 'fellow-feeling'. It is a feeling of a 'corporate sentiment of oneness'. This is one reason why a linguistic state is so essential, viz, why a state should be unilingual. There are also two other reasons why the rule 'one state, one language' is necessary to Ambedkar.[37] One, in democracy fellow-feeling is essential. Fellow-feeling in democracy is necessarily accompanied by opposition without which a democracy cannot work. But in a multilingual state, 'friction' (opposition) may be replaced by 'faction' and faction fights for leadership may bring as a result discrimination in administration. These factors are ever present in a mixed state and are incompatible with democracy.

The next reason as to why their rule be applied is that is the only solvent to racial and cultural conflicts. The different people speaking different languages when put together in a government are bound to go in different directions. Their racial and cultural interests are separate and there will be little possibility of peace between them. Therefore the mixed state is always a danger to both parties, for one may dominate the other and vice versa. Applying the same rule to Indian scenario, Ambedkar says that it would be better if India follows the road of linguistic states. However the major difficulty is that a linguistic state with its regional language may easily develop into an independent state.

Unfortunately, if this happens, India would be parceled out into a number of small states, as had happened in the medieval period. This may result into rivalry and warfare. If the whole country is divided into linguistic states, such a danger is almost certain.

Looking from this viewpoint, when Ambedkar talks of autonomy of regional cultures in the states formed on the linguistic basis and provides the unifying bond of a common national language for all the states of the Indian union, he becomes an exponent of unity in diversity. Ambedkar was always against regimentation of life and culture. His purpose, therefore, was to strengthen the social and cultural basis of Indian states with a strong feeling of nationalism. Here Ambedkar exhibits the true spirit of a nationalist when he holds: "Any Indian, who does not accept this proposal as a part and parcel of a linguistic state, has no right to be an Indian ... he cannot be an Indian in the real sense except in a geographical sense ... with regional languages as official languages and the dream to make India one united country, Indians first and Indians last will vanish.,,39 Obviously, this indicates a deep realization, on the part of Ambedkar, of the need of national integration through one common language, viz., Hindi. People through one language can exchange their views and may get themselves united for common national purposes. But it is remarkable that Ambedkar's nationalism is never incompatible with the principle that the state and government become intelligible concepts only in relation to the actual conditions of society.

Formation of Political Parties

Ambedkar's efforts to make a nation based on social amalgamation take a new tum when he chooses to institutionalize his ideas by founding a political party. He argued that political parties are essential for the working of democracy. They enable people of different opinions to agree upon some common principles, to work unitedly and secure political power by constitutional means. Dr. Ambedkar presented a descriptive and analytical definition of a political party, which said that: "A party is like an army. It must have the following characteristics - (i) A leader who is like a commander-in-chief, (ii) it must have an organization which includes (a) Membership, (b) A Ground Plan, and (c) Discipline, (iii) it must have principles and policy, (iv) it must have programs, (v) it must have strategies and tactics i.e. it must have a plan when to do what and how to reach its goal".

Having defined political party, Ambedkar goes ahead to delineate the significance of party system in parliamentary democracy and affirms that Parliamentary System of

Government is much more than Government by discussion. There are two pillars on which the Parliamentary System of Government rests. Those are the fulcrums on which this mechanism works. Those two pillars are: (i) an opposition and (ii) free and fair elections. Ambedkar proclaims, "For the last 20 to 30 years we are acclimatized to one single political party. We have nearly forgotten the necessity and importance of Opposition for the fair working of Parliamentary Democracy. We are continuously told that Opposition is an evil. Here again we are forgetting what the past history has to teach to us. You know that there were "Nibandhkaras" to interpret the Vedas and Smritis. They used to begin their comments on Slokas and Sutras by stating firstly the "Purva-Paksha", the one side of the question; they used to follow it up by giving the "Uttar Paksha", the other side. By this they wanted to show us that the question raised was not an easy question; it is a question where there is dispute, discussion and doubt. Then they used to give what they termed as Adhi Karan where they used to criticize both the Pakshas. Finally they gave the "Siddhant" - their own decision. Herefrom, we can find that all our ancient teachers believed in two party system of Government".

With these principles of a political party, Ambedkar was all set to found three significant political parties; one was named the "Independent Labor Party" in 1936 and the other was "Scheduled Castes Federation" in 1942 and lastly, the Republican Party of India in 1956. The making of ILP was formally declared on 15th August 1936, with Ambedkar himself as President and M.B. Samarath as its secretary. ILP was declared in the backdrop of Government of India Act, 1935, which envisaged representation for Indians in the Central and state legislatures on large scale. Dr. Ambedkar was prepared like others to contest elections to be held in 1937. It was the radical phase of Ambedkar when he got inclined towards Marxian class-politics. It was under the impression of class radicalism that he changed the name of his biweekly from 'Bahishkrut Bharat' to 'Janata'. Janata began to feature lead articles with large headlines targeting the atrocities of capitalists and landlords.[1]

Gail Omvedt characterizes ILP as "not a party with specific caste but rather one with a working-class identity. Its program, published in Janata, was a social democratic one, as advanced as any socialist program of the time. It accepted the 'principle of state management and ownership of industry wherever it was in the interest of the people, and it promised to amend or alter any economic system that was unjust to any class or section of the people'. It promised to bring legislation to regulate the employment of factory workers, including fixing their work-hours, making payment of adequate wages and providing bonus and pension schemes. It also promised a general scheme of social insurance. It proposed legislation to protect agricultural tenants from the exactions and evictions by landlords in general".

A close look at the programs of ILP makes us see the radical tendencies in Ambedkar as he declares also that there were two enemies of the working class in India: Brahmanism and Capitalism. To quote Ambedkar himself, "Really seen, there are only two castes in the world; the first that of the rich, and the second that of the poor. This class is responsible for the destruction of all movements".Ambedkar got disillusioned with Marxian radical tenninology, and having dissolved ILP, went on to found another political organization, named Scheduled Castes Federation, in the aftermath of Cripps Mission to India. One of the reasons behind the formation of SCF was that Ambedkar failed to see the solidarity of the working class mainly because the caste factor had diseased this class to the degree of grave ruptures, caused by caste based discrimination within the toiling classes. This led Ambedkar to believe that in free India of the future the Hindus would enjoy freedom from the British and the Muslims would secure a separate nation but the scheduled castes were still to be under the clutches of the orthodox Hindus and landlords. With this mind, he convened a meeting of the leaders of the scheduled castes all over the country to discuss the formation of a national level political party at Delhi, on 30-31 March 1942. Thus SCF became the first national political party comprising exclusively of the scheduled castes. But SCF unlike its name threw its trust fully in the principle like all Indians are equal before the law and further that it will try to minimize the gulf between the higher classes and the lower classes.

In the last year of his life Ambedkar took another step to transform his political cum electoral position from SCF to a broader category of the 'dispossessed'. With this mind he lays the foundation of the Republican Party of India which included apart from SCs, the Scheduled Tribes, Backward Classes and other minorities. In the later part of his life, Dr. Ambedkar realized that the SCF had no doubt created among the Scheduled Castes awakening for their rights and privileges, self respect, unity and strength, it had also raised a barricade between them and other classes and that old methods and outlook were incommensurable with the growing democratic consciousness of the Indian masses. Accordingly he enunciated new principles of cooperation with all, realizing further that after the independence the Federation had lost its identity and that a broad based political party was the immediate need of the hour. He, therefore, came out with the idea of dissolving the Federation and form another political party viz. 'Republican Party of India' to give it a national look, open to all, who accepted its three guiding principles viz. liberty, equality and fraternity.

The need to promote, formation and development of such a party organization - to work as an Opposition Party and to serve as basis for united political action - was engaging his attention from some time past. On November 25, 1951 speaking at a mammoth meeting of about two lakh people at Shivaji Park, Bombay, he had impressed upon them the need for an Opposition Party to build the nascent democracy in India and keep the Ruling Party in check. After a mature thought, in his last days, he unfolded his much awaited plan to the formation of the 'Republican Party of India' to bring new blood into the politics.

NATIONALISM IN DR. B.R. AMBEDKAR

Chapter 5

DR. AMBEDKAR AND NATIONALISM

Dr. Ambedkar was an iconoclastic social reformer who at the very formative years of his career realized what it meant to be an untouchable and how struggle against untouchability could be launched. The social reform movement of the caste Hindus could not win him to its side because of his existential understanding of the pangs of untouchability. The issue of untouchability, for social reformers, was a mere problem. This problem was exterior to them in the sense that it affects only the untouchables. They themselves had never experienced the sinister blows of untouchability. Though they were sympathetic to the cause of Dalits, but they belonged to the camp that imposed this inhuman system of social segregation on the Dalits.

Baba Sahib's analysis of the origins of the untouchability and his action plans for its eradication were different from the approach and practice of the caste Hindu social reformers. What distinguished Baba Sahib from the other social reformers was that he looked at the problems of the Dalits from below, from a vantage point of the deprived and oppressed. This perspective led him to think differently from the dominant stream of social and political thought of his time. His major works on: *Castes in India: Their Mechanism, Genesis and Development; Annihilation of Caste; Who Were the Shudras; The Untouchables: Who Were They and Why They Became Untouchables?* are testimonies to his independent and original thinking. He smashed the mythological basis of untouchability and laid bare its economic roots.

He built a strong case against the "*Janama*" (birth) thesis of the untouchability which foreclosed all the ways for Dalit emancipation. He exhorted its victims to oppose it tooth and nail. He said, "*It is disgraceful to live at the cost of one's self-respect. Self-respect is most vital factor in life. Without it, man is a mere cipher. To live worthily with self-respect one has to overcome difficulties. It is out of hard and ceaseless struggle alone that one derives strength, confidence and recognition*". He drew a distinction between merely living and living worthily. For living a worthy life, Ambedkar said, society must be based on liberty, equality and fraternity. For Ambedkar, social tyranny is more oppressive than the political tyranny and "*a reformer who defies society, is a much more courageous man than a politician, who defies government*".

Ambedkar was one who defied society. In the beginning of his social reform crusade, he tried to get respect and equality for the Dalits by bringing reforms within the social set up of Hinduism. He continued his struggle for empowerment of the Dalits by seeking changes within the fold of Hinduism till 1935. When he realized that the salvation of Dalits was not possible while living within the fold of Hinduism, he started his scathing criticism and tirade against Hinduism and ultimately sought the emancipation of Dalits and its empowerment from outside the Hindu religion. Hence his conversion to Buddhism. For Ambedkar the issue of Dalit liberation was the foremost issue and he emphasized that Dalits themselves have to come forward for its realization.

Thus, Ambedkar provided a subaltern perspective to see clearly the chameleon of Indian caste-ridden social set-up deceptively appearing in crimson colors and the ways to guard the interests of the Dalits.

Babasaheb Dr. B. R. Ambedkar made stringent efforts to transform the hierarchical structures of Indian society for the restoration of equal rights and justice to the neglected lot by building up a critique from within the structure of Indian society. His was not a theoretical attempt but a practical approach to the problems of untouchability. He tried to seek the solution to this perennial problem of the Indian society not by making appeals to the conscience of the usurpers or bringing transformation in the outlook of the individual by begging but by seeking transformation in the socio-religious and politico-economic structures of the Indian society by continuous and relentless struggle against the exploitative system where he thought the roots of the untouchability lay. He thought that until and unless the authority of the Dharam Shastras is shaken which provided divine sanction to the system of discrimination based on the caste hierarchy, the eradication of untouchability could not be realized. He was of the opinion that untouchability emanated neither from religious notions, nor from the much-popularised theory of Aryan conquest. On the contrary, it came into existence as a result of the struggle among the tribes at a stage when they were starting to settle down for a stable life. In the process, the settled tribes employed the broken tribesmen as guards against the marauding bands. These broken tribesmen employed as guards became untouchables.

Dr. Ambedkar's views on Indian nationalism in opposition to the dominant discourse of Hindu nationalism as represented by Raja Rammohan Roy, B.G. Tilak, Mahatma Gandhi, Jawaharlal Nehru, Golvalkar and Shyama Prasad Mookerjee on the one hand, and Communist-secular-socialist nationalism represented by M.N. Roy, R. P. Duta, T. Nagi Reddy and E.M.S. Namboodripad on the other, are not only distinct but also original. Hindu nationalism in essence aims at strengthening the Brahamanical supremacy in the post-colonial India. The communist-secular-social nationalism though based on abolition of class, its ideologues like that of the Hindu nationalism also belonged to the upper-castes and was myopic to the Dalits tribulations.

Dr. Ambedkar's conception of nationalism articulated and synthesized the national perceptions and aspirations of the downtrodden. Ambedkar's alternative form of nationalism, popularly known as Dalit-Bahujan-nationalism's incorporated the subaltern philosophy of Jyotirao Phule and Periyar E.V. Ramaswami Naicker. It constructed an anti-Hindu and anti-Brahamanical discourse of Indian nationalism. It aimed at establishing a casteless and classless society where no one would be discriminated on the basis of birth and occupation. Within the Dalit-Bahuhjan framework of Indian nationalism, Ambedkar built up a critique of pre-colonial Brahmanism and its asymmetrical social set up based on low and high dichotomy of graded caste system. This system of inegalitarianism led to the process of exploitation by the unproductive Brahamanical castes of the various productive castes.br />

Ambedkar's understanding of the question of the identity and existence of the nation was based on his incisive analysis of the oppressive character of the Hindu community. Since the dominant Hindu discourse of Indian nationalism remained indifferent towards removal of the caste system; and the economic analysis of the communist secular socialist school also failed to highlight the issue of caste in its mechanical interpretation of class, Ambedkar's himself an untouchable and victim of untouchability "*formulated his own framework from the perspective of the untouchables for the understanding of the system of caste and untouchability. The foundations of dalit-Bahujan nationalism lie in this framework developed by Ambedkar. It aimed at restructuring the Indian society into a casteless and classless and egalitarian Sangha* (Ilaiah 2001: 109)." Annihilation of caste was its central theme. Caste for Ambedkar was nothing but Brahmanism incarnate. "*Brahmanism is the poison which has spoiled Hinduism*" (Ambedkar 1995: 92). Ambedkar realised that any form of nationalism whose roots were steeped into Hinduism could not be a solution to the problem of dalits. Any discourse of nationalism bereft of annihilation of caste was just not acceptable to him. The agenda of annihilation of caste was so important to him that it became a central point of his struggle against colonial rule. In the first Round Table Conference, he minced no words in criticizing the British government for its failure to undo untouchability.

Swaraj without extinction of caste had no meaning for Ambedkar. In his undelivered speech to the Jat Pat Todak Mandal of Lahore, he said, "*In the fight for swaraj you fight with the whole nation on your side. In this, you have to fight against the whole nation and that too your own. But it is more important than swaraj. There is no use having swaraj, if you cannot defend it. More important than the question of defending swaraj is the question of defending Hindus under the swaraj. In my opinion, only when the Hindu society becomes a casteless society that it can hope to have strength enough to defend itself. Without such internal strength, swaraj for Hindus may turn out to be only a step towards slavery*". Thus, it was Ambedkar's subaltern perspective, which distinguished his conception of swaraj from that of the protagonists of the various shades of the national freedom movement. In his editorial in the *Bahishkrit Bharat*, Ambedkar wrote on 29 July 1927 "*If Tilak had been born among the untouchables, he would not have raised the slogan 'Swaraj is my birthright', but he would have raised the slogan 'Annihilation of untouchability is my birthright'*".

Ambedkar's struggle constituted a part of this internal struggle, one of the divergent and sometimes conflicting currents, all of which helped to secure 'freedom' from external and internal oppression and enslavement. Without Ambedkar's opposition to mainstream nationalism, the process of internal consolidation of the nation would not have been carried out sufficiently enough to strengthen and broaden the social base of Indian nationalism.

Ambedkar elaborated upon the idea of Nationality and Nationalism in his book 'Pakistan or the Partition of India'. He describes nationality as a, "consciousness of kind, awareness of the existence of that tie of kinship" and nationalism as "the desire for a separate national existence for those who are bound by this tie of kinship." Ambedkar had immense faith in the bright future and evolution of this country. Even when he spoke of attaining freedom for India, his ultimate goal was to unite the people.

Ambedkar was not against the idea of nationalism but against the Congress's version of it, which entailed freedom of India from British colonialism but not from Brahmanical imperialism under which millions of Scheduled Castes had been yoked for hundreds of years. It was Ambedkar's political challenge which compelled the Congress to appreciate the national significance of the problem of castes and to adopt measures which significantly contributed towards strengthening the social base of Indian nationalism.

Indian nationalism in its initial stages, by the very nature of its historical development, was an upper class (upper castes) phenomenon, reflecting the interests and aspirations of its members. Naturally when nationalists spoke in terms of national interest they certainly meant their own (class) interests. The evocation of 'nation' was a necessary ritual to ensure the much needed popular support for an essentially partisan cause. This sectarian approach to nationalism could be seen in the writings of none other than Pt. Nehru in his seminal work Discovery of India, "That mixture of religion and philosophy, history and tradition, custom and social structure, which in its wide fold included almost every aspect of the life of India, and which might be called Brahminism or Hinduism, became the symbol of nationalism. It was indeed a national religion."

The sectarian character of Indian nationalism persisted even after the nascent upper castes' movement developed into a truly mass-supported anti-imperialist national liberation movement. And, it is because of this failure to change its basically pro-upper class/castes orientation that the Indian national movement in due course helped the rise of new parallel sectarian socio-political currents. Ambedkar's emergence on the Indian political scene in 1920s, commencing the advent of Dalit (the scheduled castes) politics, was simply the manifestation of the same process.

At that time, Ambedkar's Dalit politics posed no really significant threat to the overall domination of the traditional ruling class, yet it exposed the hollowness of the Congress's claim to represent the whole nation. The nationalist leadership remained unwilling to attack long unresolved social contradictions at the base of the Hindu social order and propelled people like Ambedkar to contest the INC's claim that it represented the whole society.

It was in the backdrop of this escapism of the Congress brand of nationalism that an alternative subaltern nationalism was born through Ambedkar. Ambedkar took up this question from the 'social below' and brought it to a political high by linking the question of caste with that of democracy and nationalism. Such an effort to prioritise society over polity and then linking them together was unprecedented in India before Ambedkar. Gandhi can be said to have made such an effort but his approach was obscure and primitive.

There is no doubt that Ambedkar was vehemently opposed to unjust social stratification in India, but to say that he was against the nation is wrong. He was definitely against the Congress version of Nationalism. Ambedkar was neither an anti-national nor just a leader of the Scheduled Castes. He was a national leader who understood the problems of the most exploited communities and tried to bring them into the main stream. He expanded the social base of Indian nationalism which helped first to attain freedom and later to put the country on path of progress. Today, when all thought converges around inclusive politics, Ambedkar has become more relevant than ever.

DR. B.R. AMBEDKAR'S IDEA OF NATIONALISM IN THE CONTEXT OF INDIA'S FREEDOM MOVEMENT

This section analyses the self generated vision of Ambedkar regarding nationalism critically. Nationalism is an ideology based on devotion to love of one s country either by birth or by choice which focuses upon the attitude that the members of a nation have when they care about their national identity and actions that the members of a nation take when seeking to achieve some form of political sovereignty. Nationalism, in a wider sense, is any complex of attitudes, claims and directives for action ascribing a fundamental political, moral, cultural value to nations and nationality and deriving special obligations and permissions from this ascribed value. Nationalism in Ambedkar initiated to object internal oppression as well as external domination. He wanted equality and civil rights for those who for centuries deprived of them. Indian society, in view of Ambedkar, was a system which gave no scope for the growth of the sentiment of equality and fraternity which are essential for a democratic form of government. Many people were deprived of the basic human rights. He wanted constitutional safeguards to protect oppressed. Ambedkar was of the outlook that Indian society was nothing but gradation of caste which consists of ascending scale of reverence and descending scale of contempt. Ambedkar s view was very transparent regarding foreign domination. Ambedkar viewed that inspite of realizing the necessity of removing some social evils which had horrified the lives of down- trodden people, British attitude was indifferent in eradicating some social evils simply because of the reason that its intervention in the-then existing code of social and economic life would give rise to resistance. Ambedkar s spirit of nationalism took a proper shape through the struggle against such British rule although foreign rule had been the potential force in the country like India.

Nationalism in Ambedkar stems from his spirit of dignity both for the people and for the country. He had profound feeling for the poor and untouchables which induced him to fight against denial of basic human rights. Such attitudes of Ambedkar were called by some congress leader as anti-national, but in true sense, it was nothing but expression of humanism and nationalism to which he sincerely devoted himself.

Those who blamed Ambedkar for his opposition to congress-led freedom struggle failed to understand that freedom from alien rule was no more significant than freedom from internal form of slavery and exploitation. To Ambedkar, if freedom of a country cannot be distinguished from freedom of its people, true freedom would be misleading concept. To him, „„philosophically, it may be possible to consider a nation as a unit but sociologically, it cannot be regarded as consisting of many classes and freedom of the nation, if it is to be a reality, must vouchsafe the freedom of the different classes comprised in it, particularly of those who are treated as the servile classes". In true sense, Ambedkar gave due weight age on the emancipation of oppressed people who for years remained enslaved by *Varna Hindus*. If nation is to be considered as co-extensive with the ruling class, it is to be truly representative of all people. This is only possible when these people are quite free from fear, oppression and exploitation resulting real freedom of the people. According to Ambedkar, a nation consists of whole society i.e. groups and classes , varied ranges of life in one hand and on the other hand area of soil which is the physical features of the land this social classes occupy . He laid stress on the freedom of people, although he did not have any contrary view regarding India s physical freedom. This created a misunderstanding in the mind of those who could not make such a distinction between these two things. It is well- known that nationalist leader in general and the Hindu nationalists in particular laid excessive emphasis on the political freedom ignoring the social aspects of nationalism. Ambedkar s argument was that in the absence of complete freedom of the people, nationalism becomes a conduit of internal slavery, organized tyranny for the poor and depressed classes.

In view of Ambedkar, nationalism means expression of inner unity of a people and it is a process of social assimilation. Therefore, irrespective of caste, colour and creed, nationalism gets perfect harmony if social brotherhood of men prevails everywhere within a nation. To Ambedkar, nationalism is negation of caste spirit and caste spirit is nothing but deep-rooted communalism. He emphasized to fight against casteism, linguism, communalism and separatism because he was of the opinion that these social evils divide the people into small social units which are against the spirit of nationalism. In view of Ambedkar, communalism being one form of groupism is a threat to national integration which may hamper the way for equally and fraternity. In short, Ambedkar viewed nationalism as a spiritual phenomenon rooted in humanism.

Ambedkar s view of nationalism and patriotism creates a strong sense of social brotherhood in doing justice and good to the needy, lowly who live in the same country but are not treated as full man. Ordinarily, nationalism is a feeling of attachment to national society whereas patriotism is a feeling of attachment to the very soil of the "land of our birth" . To Ambedkar, patriotism and nationalism are of utmost need for democracy and equality. Ambedkar s view regarding this is that patriotism demand action in right direction and reaction against all wrong and a nationalist leader should have deep faith in himself to eradicate imperialism, social tyranny, casteism, communalism, forced labour etc. In a word, Ambedkar s idea of nationalism creates a spirit of social brotherhood, feeling of oneness and a firm determination to improve the lot of people who remain oppressed in the same country.

Ambedkar, the believer of one nationalism, advocates for religious tolerance and condemns all kinds of hypocrisy and oppression in the name of religion and nationalism. Amidst diversity of religions in Indian nation, he aspires that "religion should be the force which deepens the solidarity of human society" which can bring people together for social and emotional unity, can lead the people to military unity and political stability. To him, "the divine right of the majority to rule the minorities according to the wishes of the majority" is an example of irrationalism and such monopoly of power and prestige by majority religious or political group is not nationalism, rather anti- nationalism. Accepting different religions in Indian society having religious differences, Ambedkar believes that these religions should be binding forces behind creating national spirit and in no situation, these religions should be a symbol of inhuman treatment and ignominy. Otherwise, it will hamper the development of strong sense of national unity.

Recognizing the demerits of diversity of language in a country, Ambedkar opined that different language should not obstruct the growth and spirit of nationalism and in favour of his opinion, he cited examples of Canada, Switzerland and South Africa which have diversified languages. Yet, Ambedkar laid stresses on the need of a common language in order to strengthen the unity and spirit of nationalism as well as to remove racial and cultural conflicts. Through one common language, Ambedkar wanted to have a strong sense of unity and a deep feeling of nationalism. He had the arguments in support of his claim that people speaking different languages might not be able to exchange thoughts and actions for development and happiness of all men irrespective of race, caste and religion. Moreover, one language could not only tighten the sense of human unity in a nation but also remove racial and cultural tension.

The indifferent attitude of British towards establishing social equality and civic liberty made Ambedkar very much vocal. The spirit of strong nationalism roused in him to struggle against foreign rule with a view to bring freedom for men as well as to restore rights of the depressed classes. In view of Ambedkar , unless and until the Indian people secure political power and unless that power was concentrated in the hands of the socially suppressed section of the Indian society , it would not be possible to completely eradicate all social , legal and cultural disabilities under which that section suffered. He was not only against British imperialism but also advocated for self Government. As a result, he said „We must have a government in which the men in power will give their undivided allegiance to the best interest of the country. In Ambedkar s political thought, it is explicitly apparent that he attempted to awaken social and national consciousness against British neutralism which proved fatal to the social emancipation of people.

Though nationality and nationalism are two different psychological states of human mind, there can not be nationalism without the feeling of nationality. In view of Ambedkar, nationality is ' a feeling of consciousness of kind which is on one hand binds together to those who have it , so strongly that it overrides all differences arising out of economic conflicts or social gradations and on the other hand , severs them from those who are not their kind . It is a feeling not to belong to any other group. This is the essence of what is called a nationality and national feeling . He opined that nationality may turn into nationalism when two conditions are satisfied :

a) There must arise the desire to live as a nation and nationalism is a dynamic expression of that desire.

b) There must be a territory which nationalism could occupy and make it a state as well as a cultural home of the nation . Therefore, Ambedkar is of the opinion that nationalism should be based on a strong will to live as a nation and deep feeling to make a state or cultural home with definite territory. Political unity will not alone bring about such kind of nationalism rather social unity would be more congenial for bringing about a sense of human brotherhood which induces a sense of oneness. In order to bring about a sense of human brotherhood, Ambedkar laid stress on spiritual unity of the people regardless of communal inhibition and discouraged all kinds of heterogeneity, doubts and differences. With the object of establishing all-round harmony among the people, spiritual harmony was thought to be much nobler task to him than making conflict with British Government. Ambedkar warned people against the spirit of blind hero- worship because he thought that the service to the people of a nation is nobler than the worship of political heroes. He was of the opinion that „*Bhakti'* is a path to the salvation of the soul, but in politics, *Bhakti* or hero worship is a sure road to degradation and eventual dictatorship. He has argument in support of his opinion that the worship of political heroes has killed public conscience because the heroes think only of their worshippers and neglect the common cause of mankind . Rather, he attempted to solve the political, social and religious problems of India through his democratic humanistic method. Though educated and impressed by western culture, he laid stress on the need of cultural regeneration preserving the best elements of our culture and civilization.

Within Ambedkar s thought, the concept as well as the reality of nation looms very large. Nation is an ideal- typical construct, a social category built around certain principles. A serious and ideological commitment engendering an equally serious change in social and societal relations at least is a necessary prerequisite to actualize the nation as a political entity. In the concrete of the subcontinent, this demands that caste in all its dimensions, both the system and spirit whether understood in its pristine *vedic- shastraic purity* or in its degraded and distorted nineteenth -century form, be renounced once and for all as an ideology and principle of social order and organization; and socio- politically move towards and aspire to another form of society and social relations. This ideological renunciation and a „re-socialization is the condition for the desire to constitute an independent polity.

Nationalism for Ambedkar is „ the desire for a separate national existence for those bound by this tie of kinship. It is a will to live as a nation in the full sense of the term not only socially but also politically. Nationalism as an ideology and a movement succeeds the nation as the corporate feeling. It is a praise-worthy desire for those bound by this tie of kinship. Ambedkar is categorically on this point: „there cannot be nationalism without the feeling of nationality in existence . It is precisely this feeling of corporate and communicative oneness that legitimizes the demand for self-determination and then the claim for nation-statehood becomes irresistible.

Within the small group of marginalized intellectuals who have kept the flame of thoughts of Ambedkar alive with regard to nationalism , they all also remain to be defensive protesting that Babasaheb Ambedkar also was national in the same sense or within the same nationalist paradigm as that of the mainstream leaders that Ambedkar too was anti- British, that he also desired independence as an absolute value and that he considered when compared to *swarjya* beneficial to the masses , particularly the lower castes. Therefore, comparing with the onslaught of the dominant ideology of the nationalist leaders, Ambedkar s nationalism and patriotism in the traditional sense could not be made to appear vibrant.Nationalism in Ambedkar began in protest both against external domination and internal oppression. Indian society, according to him, was a gradation of castes forming an ascending scale of reverence and descending scale of contempt.To Ambedkar, Gandhiji s aim in joining the temple entry movement was to destroy the basis of the claim of the untouchables for political rights by destroying the barrier between them and the Hindus which made them separate from the Hindus. He characterized Gandhiji s temple entry movement as a strange game of political acrobatics. The indifferent attitude of British towards establishing social equality and civic liberty made Ambedkar very much vocal. Hindu had to lose much by the abolition of untouchability. The system of untouchability was a gold mine to the Hindus. In this society, there was a master class and a servile class. Untouchability was more than a religious system. It was an economic system which was worse than slavery .Hindus belonged to the exploiting class where Hindus gained economic advantage by perpetuating untouchability. He thought that in *Swaraj*, the untouchables would get no privileges but the perpetuation of slavery. He was not only against British imperialism but also advocated for self Government. He had realized that nationality had a most intimate connection with the claim for self-government. He knew that by the end of the 19th century, it had became an accepted principle that the people, who constituted a nation, were entitled on that account to self- government and that any patriot, who asked for self-government for his people, had to prove that they were a nation. He never cared to reason whether nationality was merely a question of calling a people a nation or was a question of the people being a nation.

THE RELATION BETWEEN DEMOCRACY AND NATIONALISM IN AMBEDKAR

Ambedkar's notion of a democratic nation and nationalism appears to be quite unprecedented on Indian subcontinent in colonial era. The genesis of both the terms 'Democracy' and 'Nation' lies in Europe and the rest of the world have imported them as per their needs and suitability. But European society unlike Indian society was never in the trap of socially ascriptive hierarchy (Caste division) and therefore, in spite of the early emergence of a plethora of theories in Europe on "Democracy" and "Nationalism", the caste question was never included. European and even American theories of *democracy* and *nationalism* dealt with only those questions of primordial identities which their societies were faced with, for instance, race, religion, minority rights and so on rather than caste. The whole question of caste as a socio-political problem remained specific to India for which Europe and America had no answer at least in colonial period.

Gandhi took up the *Caste Question* in the reformist and status quoist manner by conserving the Varna system and the Congress socialists suppressed the question itself by not regarding it worth discussing and instead preferred to discuss and govern through rather refined European ideologies. Congress nationalism therefore could be recriminated of neglecting this question persistently. It was in the backdrop of this escapist attitude of Congress nationalism that an alternative subalternist political nationalism was born in Ambedkar. Ambedkar took up this question from social below and elevated it to political high by linking this social question of caste with the political question of democracy and nationalism. Such an effort to prioritize society over polity and then linking them together was unprecedented in India before Ambedkar. Gandhi can be said to have made such an effort but his approach was obscure and primitive as it ended up in anarchy wherein society would self-sufficiently continue without any need for state.

To elaborate further, in the political realm, Ambedkar's nationalism begins with the French revolutionary spirit of 'Liberty', 'Equality' and 'Fraternity'. But he extends his national spirit beyond the political realm down to the larger social realm and takes pain to reconcile the two distinct realms within the limits of the democratic structure. In the social realm he takes inspiration from the Lord Buddha to explain the optimum of liberty and equality. Using his own terminology, he defines law in terms of having a place only as a safeguard against the breaches of liberty and equality rather than as a guarantee for breaches of liberty and equality.} In his own conceptual perspective of socially-inclusive nationalism, he takes 'social-change' as the sole means to meet this end and thus be seen as a champion of *neglected humanity*.

The argument between the liberals and the liberals-turned-democrats was over whether the male poor would use their rights to strip the rich of their wealth, or whether they would leave decision making to the middle rank - whom James Mill described as the class in society which gives to science, art and legislation their most 'distinguished ornaments' and is the chief source of all that is 'refined and exalted in human nature'. Both sides of the argument agreed that the business of government is the business of the rich (Hoffman, 1988: 167). The question of exclusion becomes more subtle as liberals become more enthusiastic about the idea of democracy. T. H. Green and Leonard Hobhouse, two British social liberals, both supported the idea that women as well as men should have the voting right. But Green could still take it for granted that men were the head of the family, and Hobhouse argued that women should stay at home and mind the children Both J .S. Mill and de Tocqueville raised the problem of democracy as a 'tyranny of the majority'. These writers were pioneers, for sure, in deliberating upon the question how a government representing the majority should be prevented from crushing a minority? Crick endorses what has been called a 'paradox of freedom' - a situation in which an elected leader acts tyrannically towards particular individuals or groups. To escape from such situations, new liberals like Hobhouse argued that checks should be placed upon the British House of Commons to restrain 'a large and headstrong majority'

Towards the end of World War II the concept of democracy was redefined, in order to bring it into line, so it was emphatically argued, with practical realities. Joseph Schumpeter, an Austrian economist and socialist, led the way, contending that the notion of democracy must be stripped of its moral qualities. There is nothing about the democracy that makes it desirable. It may be that in authoritarian systems - Schumpeter gives the example of the religious settlement under the military dictatorship of Napoleon I - the wishes of the people are more fully realized than under a democracy

In Schumpeter's view, democracy is simply a 'political method'. It is an arrangement for reaching political decisions: it is not an end in itself. Since all governments 'discriminate' against some section of the population (in no political system are children allowed to vote, for example), discrimination as such is not undemocratic. It all depends upon how the demos or the people are defined. Schumpeter admits that in contemporary liberal societies all adults should have the right to vote, but this does not mean that they will use this right or participate more directly in the political process. In fact, he argues that it is a good idea if the mass of the population do not participate, since the masses are too irrational, emotional, parochial and 'primitive' to make good decisions. The typical citizen, he argues, yields to prejudice, impulse and what Schumpeter calls 'dark urges'. It is the politicians, who raise the issues that determine people's lives, and who decide these issues. A democracy is more realistically defined as 'political method' through which politicians are elected by means of a competitive vote. The people do not rule: their role is to elect those who do. Democracy is a system of elected and competing elites. The 1950s saw a number of studies which argued that politics is a remote, alien and unrewarding activity best left to a relatively small number of professional activists. The model of elitist democracy, as it has sometimes been called, argued the case for a democracy with low participation.

But sooner than later, the view of "Low Participation" came under an all round attack by the participatory democrats arguing that low participation undermines democracy. In his *Life and Times of Liberal Democracy* Macpherson sets about constructing a participatory model, arguing that somehow participatory democrats have to break the vicious circle between an apathy which leads to inequality (as the poor and vulnerable lose out), and inequality that generates apathy (as the poor and vulnerable feel impotent and irrelevant). Macpherson's argument is an interesting one, as he takes the view that one needs to start with people as they are. Participatory democrats began to redefine, in broader terms, participation and democracy above the level of franchise. They began to ponder over other forms of participation in a democracy, for instance, even the person who does not vote may join, say, Anmesty Intemational or Greenpeace in Britain. There is an argument for increasing the number of people who vote in parliamentary elections or what they call 'compulsory voting' which is also regarded as extension of universal franchise. Simultaneously, some bring our attention to democratic participation at different levels and in different ways. The large numbers of people who turned out to protest against the war with Iraq in London and other places showed that a lack of concern with politics can be exaggerated, and the rise of what are usually called the New Social Movements - single issue organizations concerned with peace, the environment, rights of women, etc. - indicate that there is increasing participation, even if some of this participation seems unconventional in character.

Contriving Ambedkar's Theory of Democracy

Before adding his neology to the concept of 'Democracy', Ambedkar puts forth two already prevailing views of 'Democracy'; one view is that 'Democracy' is a form of government. According to this view, where the government is chosen by the people that is where government is a representative government, there is 'Democracy'. According to this view 'Democracy' is just synonymous with representative government which means adult suffrage and periodical elections. According to another view a democracy is more than a form of government. It is a form of the organization of society.3 There are two essential conditions, which characterize a democratically constituted society. First is the absence of stratification of society into classes. The second is a social habit on the part of individuals and groups, which is ready for continuous readjustment or recognition of reciprocity of interests. As to the first, there can be no doubt, Ambedkar mentions, that it is the most essential condition of 'Democracy'. The second condition is equally necessary for a democratically constituted society. The results of this lack of reciprocity of interests among groups and individuals produce anti-democratic structures and negate the very purpose of 'Democracy'.

Judging both the views of 'Democracy', Ambedkar states that there is no doubt that the first one is very superficial if not erroneous. There cannot be democratic government unless the society for which it functions is democratic in its form and structure. Ambedkar believes that those who hold that democracy need be no more than a mere matter of elections make three mistakes. One mistake they make is to believe that government is something which is quite distinct and separate from society. While as a matter of fact government is not something which is distinct and separate from society; government is one of the many institutions which society rears and to which it assigns the function of carrying out some of the duties which are necessary for collective social life.

The second mistake they make, Ambedkar believes, lies in their failure to realize that a government is to reflect the ultimate purposes, aims, objects and wishes of society and this can happen only where the society in which the government is rooted is democratic. If society is not democratic, government can never be; where society is divided into two classes governing and the governed, the government is bound to be the government of the governing class. The third mistake they make is to forget that whether government would be good or bad, democratic or undemocratic depends to a large extent upon the instrumentalities particularly the civil-service on which everywhere government has to depend for administering the law. It all depends upon the social milieu in which civil-servants are nurtured. If the social milieu is undemocratic, the government is bound to be undemocratic. There is another possible mistake which is responsible for the view that for democracy to function it is enough to have a democratic form of government. To realize this mistake, cites Ambedkar, it is necessary to have some idea of what is meant by good government. Responding to the same, he asserts that good government means good laws and good administration. This is the essence of good government. Now there cannot be good government in this sense if those who are invested with ruling power seek the advantage of their own class instead of the advantage of the whole people or downtrodden.

On the way to examine the ideal form of democracy, Ambedkar lays considerable stress upon individual subjective morality. He argues further that whether the democratic form of government results in good-will would depend upon the disposition of the individuals composing society. If the mental disposition of the individuals is democratic then the democratic form of government can be expected to result in good government. If not, democratic form of government may easily become a dangerous form of government. Ambedkar begins to look for the necessity of the individual bent -of-mind to be healthy enough to practice political democracy on the one hand and at the same time availability of the proper social milieu to shape the individual psyche in its classless form. Thereafter he strives to link the individual psyche to that of social milieu in a fashion so as to verify that the democratic attitude of mind is the conditional end-product of the prerequisite socialization of the individual in a democratic society. Democratic society is, therefore, a prerequisite of a democratic government. Democratic governments have toppled down largely due to the fact that the society for which they were set up was not democratic. To quote Prof. Rodrigues in this respect, "He did not reconcile the tension between democracy and law and in his exposition, the domain of reason and morals are often in contention with that of law. Ideally, of course, he envisaged a democracy informed by law and a law characterized by sensitivity to democracy. At the same time he looked to a system of law which upheld reason and morality, though he saw reason and morality as far too feeble to ensure social bonds without the authoritative dictates expressed in law. Religion, according to him, could play a major role in lightening the task of law. Ambedkar's views on constitutional democracy were reflected in his relations with Gandhi and Nehru on the issues of untouchability and the Hindu Code Bill respectively.

On the evening of October 27, 1951, after inaugurating the election campaign at Jalandhar, Dr. Ambedkar had addressed a special session of the "Political Scientists Parliament" of the D.A.V. College. Speaking on the occasion he sounded a note of warning that if Parliamentary Democracy fails in this country - and it is bound to fail because of the attitude of the party in power - rebellion, anarchy and communism will be the only result. Then the fate of this country will be doomed. Speaking at length he cited many rules about Parliamentary Procedure - elaborating, "That at one time India had parliamentary institutions and that there are innumerable references in our literature to prove that Parliamentary System of Government was not unknown to us - that Parliamentary Government means negation of hereditary rule. No person can claim to be a hereditary ruler. Whosoever wants to rule must be elected by the people from time to time. He must obtain approval of the people. Hereditary rule has no sanction in the Parliamentary System of Government".

Again adding to the same, he continues, "Secondly, any law, any measure applicable to the public life of the people must be based on the advice of the people chosen by the people. No single individual can presume the authority that he knows everything, that he can make the laws and carry the Government. The laws are to be made by the representatives of the people in the Parliament. They are the people who can advise the man in whose name the law is proclaimed. Thirdly, Parliamentary System of Government means that at a stated period those who want to advise the Head of the State must have the confidence of the people in themselves renewed".

Further he continues, "One important thing in the Parliamentary Democracy is that people should know the other side if there are two sides to a question. Hence a functional opposition is required. Opposition is the key to a free political life. No democracy can do without it. Britain and Canada, the two exponents of Parliamentary System of Government recognize this important fact and in both countries the leader of the Opposition is paid salary by the Government. They regard the Opposition as an essential thing. People of these countries believe that the Opposition should be as much alive as the Government. The Government may suppress the facts;

the Government may have only one- sided propaganda. The people have made provision against this eventuality in these two countries. A free and fair election is the other pillar on which Parliamentary Democracy rests. Free and fair elections are necessary for the transfer of power from one section of the community to the other in a peaceful manner and without any bloodshed. People must be left to themselves to choose those whom they want to send to the Legislatures"

Fraternity in Hinduism

Ambedkar feels strongly that the Hindu religion does not teach fraternity. Instead it teaches division of society into classes or Varnas and the maintenance of separate class-consciousness. Above all, the Hindu social system is undemocratic not by accident, but it is designed to be undemocratic. Its division of society into Varnas and castes and of castes and outcastes are not theories but decrees. They are all barricades raised against democracy. From this it would appear that the doctrine of fraternity was unknown to the Hindu religious and philosophic thought. But such a conclusion, affirms Ambedkar, would not be warranted by the facts of history.

Hinduism offers two contradictory theories of its structure. One is 'theory of Varna' based on hierarchical inequality which is also in universal practice in India. Another is the doctrine of *'Brahmaism'*, which is largely hidden and confined to the texts only. Ambedkar brings to light the fact that this doctrine of Brahmaism has greater potentialities for producing social democracy than the Western idea of fraternity. This might appear strangely new even to the Hindus as they are not familiar with 'Brahmaism' as they are with 'Brahamanism' which are two separate ideological pillars of Hinduism. The essence of 'Brahmaism' is summed up by Ambedkar as follows:

(i) All this is Brahma.

(ii) Self is the same as Brahma. Therefore I am Brahma.

(iii) Self is the same as Brahma. Therefore you are also Brahma.

Ambedkar is of the opinion that most people know the distinction between the Vedanta and Brahmanism, but very few people know the distinction between Brahmaism and Vedanta, even the Hindus are not aware of it. But the distinction is noteworthy; while Brahmaism and Vedanta agree that Atman/self is the same as Brahma. But the two differ sharply in that Brahmaism does not treat the world as unreal, Vedanta does. This is the fundamental difference between the two. The essence of Brahmaism is that the world is real and the reality behind the world is Brahma. Everything therefore is the essence of Brahma. Ambedkar scrutinizes the criticisms leveled against Brahmaism. It is said that Brahmaism is a piece of impudence. For a man to say "I am Brahma" is a kind of arrogance. The other criticism leveled against Brahmaism is the inability of man to know Brahma.

Ambedkar counters the criticism by saying that 'I am Brahma' may appear to be impudence, but it can also be an assertion of one's worth. In a world where humanity suffers so much from an inferiority complex such an assertion on the part of man is to be welcomed. Democracy demands that each individual shall have every opportunity for realizing its worth. It also requires that each individual shall know that he is as good as everybody else. Those, who sneer at 'I am Brahma' as an impudent utterance, forget the other part of the Mahavakya, namely "Thou art also Brahma". Thus the criticism of selfish arrogance leveled against Brahmaism does not hold ground. This theory of Brahma has certain social implications which, to Ambedkar, have a tremendous value as a foundation for democracy. If all persons are parts of Brahma then all are equal and all must enjoy the same liberty which is what democracy means.

To support democracy, as Christians say, because we are all children of God, is a very weak foundation for democracy to rest on. That is why democracy is so shaky wherever it is made to rest on such a foundation. But to recognize and realize that you and 1 are parts of the same cosmic principle leaves room for no other theory of associated life except democracy. It does not merely preach democracy; it makes democracy an obligation of one and all. Ambedkar mocks at the western students of democracy who have spread the belief that democracy has stemmed either from Christianity or from Plato and that there is no other source of inspiration for democracy. But if they had known, Ambedkar exhibits his nationalism, that India too had developed the doctrine of Brahmaism, which furnishes a better foundation for democracy, they would not have been so dogmatic. India too must be admitted, he declares, to have made a contribution towards a theoretical foundation for democracy. But when it comes to praxis, he gets disappointed because in everyday customary practice Brahmaism has been without doubt overtaken by the force of Brahmanism. As to why Brahmaism failed to produce a new society, Ambedkar says, it is a great riddle ... and regrettable truth that has carried no social effect and died in philosophy.

Correlating Nationalism and Democracy

According to Ambedkar, 'nationalism' in relation to a nation should be based on a strong feeling of social unity and in relation to 'internationalism', the human brotherhood. And such nationalism, fraught with the spirit of democracy, would not base itself upon a tyranny nor would it ever be a menace to any community and nation. There is a distinction between a community and a nation. Ambedkar quotes Sidgewick on the distinction between the two: 'A community has a right to safeguard; a nation has a right to demand separation'.

In this regard, the subtle distinctions, to Ambedkar's acumen, between 'nationality' and 'nation' must be noted down. While 'nationality' implies "consciousness of kin, awareness of the existence of that tie of kinship; 'nationalism' implies the desire for a separate national existence for those who are bound by this tie of kinship". Nationalism, to Ambedkar, cannot exist without the feeling of nationality.

However, nationality does not in all cases produce nationalism. Here Oneil Biswas finds two points worth mentioning: first, nationality is a dynamic expression of the desire to live as a nation; and secondly that there ought to be a territory which nationalism can occupy and make it a state and also a cultural home of the nation?

Ambedkar also goes ahead to draw a line between the freedom of the country and freedom of the people and it is the latter which is more important of the two. Thus he takes pain to exhibit that without the freedom of the people, nationalism becomes a means of internal/domestic slavery, forced labor and organized tyranny for the poor and servile classes. According to him, "it is entirely wrong to concentrate all our attention on the political independence of our country, and to forget the far more serious problem of social and economic independence. It is suicidal to imagine that political independence necessarily means real all-sided freedom"

Ambedkar stressed the need for fighting against provincialism, linguism, casteism and communalism. Casteism operated in particular against nationalism and he asserts that caste ism has killed public- spirit. It has destroyed the sense of public charity and made public opinion impossible, virtue has become caste-ridden, and morality caste-bound. To him, nationalism meant the negation of caste-spirit which was another name for deep-rooted communalism. But unfortunately in India nationalism took a new turn in terms of majority and minority rule with a vengeance so as to boss over the minorities. Be exposed all kinds of hypocrisy and oppression in the name of religion and nationalism. Since India is not a nation but each caste is, the preamble to the constitution of India, starts with the expression, *"We, the People of India"*, some politicians objected to it in the Constituent Assembly debate and preferred "The Indian Nation". Ambedkar replied to this by asking how people divided into several thousands of castes could be a nation. And he also warned that the sooner we realize that we are not as yet a nation in the social and psychological sense of the word, the better for us.

Apart from the socio-political aspects of nationalism, Ambedkar, being a realist in his approach, was very much aware of the fact that any nationalism based on social justice would remain a myth if not linked legally to constitutional forces. Keeping it in mind, Ambedkar took all the pains to translate his notion of social justice and nationalism into legal terminology. Justice K. Ramaswamy while probing into the legal aspects of nationalism likes to call Ambedkar a true democrat, a nationalist to the core and a patriot of highest order on various grounds. He was the author and principal actor to make the 'Directi ve Principles' as part of the constitutional scheme. When it was criticized that the directive principles could not be enforced in a court of law, and hence there would be no need to have them incorporated in the Constitution, Ambedkar answered that though they were not enforceable, the succeeding majority political party in Parliament or Legislative Assembly would be bound by them as an inbuilt part of their economic programme in the governance, despite their policy in its manifesto and are bound by the Constitution?5 Ambedkar, in his Constitutional schema of nationalism, undertook the task of strengthening the Executive in particular and the notion of 'Integrated Bharat' in general.

Uniform Civil Code

Rising above the regional, linguistic and communal barriers in a true republican spirit, Ambedkar invents a democratic nationalism consisting of uniform civil code for India if it aspires nationhood. His views of Uniform Civil Code was radically different from his contemporaries including Nehru who in principles accepted Hindu Code Bill and Uniform Civil Code but in practice, failed to get the Bill passed at one go, in spite of being in Government with majority. Ambedkar on the other hand made it a point to add the word 'fraternity' in the Preamble to the Constitution in order to inculcate the sense of common brotherhood of aU Indians, of Indians being one people; it is the principle which gives unity and solidarity to social life.

In the Constituent Assembly Debates, while speaking on the *Hindu Code Bill* he urged the Members to have a common code which would do away with unequal rules of Hindu law scattered in immovable decisions of the High Courts and of the Privy Council, motley of seven different matters - Right of property of a deceased Hindu to both male and female, the order of succession to the different heirs of the proEerty, the law of maintenance, marriage, divorce, adoption, minority and guardianship. 6 With regard to inter- caste and inter-sub- caste marriages and adherence of monogamy, Ambedkar made it clear that monogamous marriage had been prevalent since the time of Kautilya and second marriage was permissible only in exceptional circumstances. About ninety percent of the people had customary divorce. Therefore, according to the new principles of inter-caste marriages, monogamy and introductions of divorce under the Hindu Code Bill were reasonable and just supported not only by the precedents but also by the world as a whole. Ambedkar notes that after it comes into operation, any two Hindus irrespective of caste and faith may solemnize marriage under the Hindu Marriage Act, 1955. Thus a Shudra can validly marry a Brahmin or a Rajput or a Sikh girl.

At the same time, he was also critical of Muslim Personal Law and tried his best to abolish it in favor of Uniform Civil Code. Ambedkar did not agree to the fact that Muslims had any immutable and uniform laws in India up to 1935. The Shariat Law did not apply to the North-West Frontier provinces. It followed the Hindu Law of succession and other matters so much so that in 1939 the Central Legislature had come into the field to abrogate the application of Hindu Law to the Muslims of North-West provinces and to apply Shariat Law to them. The same was true of Muslims in various parts of the United Provinces, Central Provinces and Bombay where Muslims were largely governed by the Hindu Law of succession. In North Malabar, the Murumakkathayam, a matriarchal law of succession applied commonly to both Hindus and Muslims. That was the reason that Muslim elites persuaded the British Government and ultimately the Shari at Act, 1937, was enacted. Ambedkar emphasized that in a secular state religion should not be allowed to govern all human activities and that Personal Laws should be divorced from religion.

To quote Ambedkar on Personal Laws, "If a saving clause were introduced into the Constitution it would disable the legislature in India from enacting any social measure whatsoever. The religious conceptions in this country are so vast that they cover every aspect of life from birth to death. There is nothing which is not religious and if Personal Law is to be saved, I am sure about it that in social matters we will come to a standstill. I do not think that it is possible to accept a position of that sort. In Europe, there is Christianity but Christianity does not mean that the Christians all over the world or in any part of Europe where they live shall have a uniform inheritance law. No such thing exists. I personally do not understand that religion should be given this vast expensive jurisdiction so as to cover the whole of life and to prevent the legislature from encroaching upon that field. After all, what we are having this liberty for? We are having this liberty in order to reform our social system, which is so full of inequities, so full of inequalities, discriminations and other things, which conflict with our fundamental rights. It is, therefore, quite impossible for anybody to conceive that the Personal Laws should be excluded from the jurisdiction of the state".28 Thus Ambedkar believed that there is no legal bar in enacting a Unifonn Civil Code by the Legislatures even if Article 35 is not adopted in the Constitution.

Taking a feminist perspective on the question of citizenship and uniform civil code, Nivedita Menon argues that citizenship is super homogenous identity which deprives a citizen of all of its distinguishing marks including that of sex and by this virtue this domain is no more inherently emancipatory than the domain of premodern 'fuzzy boundaries' (Menon borrows this phrase from Sudipta Kaviraj). Nivedita Menon seems to belong to that school of theorists who are not comfortable with the very idea of 'nationalism', 'citizenship' and 'UCC' and would prefer to abandon these ideas completely in favor of 'community rights' provided a community promises to deliver on the issue of 'gender-equality'. She criticizes Partha Chatterjee for giving an absolutist authority to the community which virtually means "authority to the males of the given community to decide on behalf of females". Partha Chatterjee surely gives clean chit not only to the patriarchal forces of the community but also to the ruling elites of the same community to decide on behalf of others and in the interests of themselves when he holds that a collective cultural right is in fact the 'right not to offer a reason for being different'.

If we bring in Ambedkar's notion of nationalism, citizenship and uniform civil code at this juncture, we would note that Ambedkar's point of departure is also difference-based community rights but simultaneously he also takcs care of the fact that these differential group-rights must be reconciled to the larger idea of citizenship and nationalism. Ambedkar was also largely concemed with the issue of social -reforms and if religious personal laws come on the way to social refonns, he would rather go for the social reforms even at the expense of personal laws. This is evident from the fact that on the question of Partition, Ambedkar was of the opinion that Muslims must be allowed to make a separate nation, not in so much because they have been a separate nation in India but chiefly because they want to become a separate nation and hence their will to become a separate nation must be respected.

Should be made available to any person on demand, no matter what community he or she may belong to. This would also mean that the state machinery is not made available for implementing any religious laws - Hindu, Muslim or Christian. Equal rights for women should be the underlying principle for such a code. The Muslim leadership, he argues, cannot legitimately oppose the right of voluntary choice. This also implies that the codified Hindu law as incorporated in the Hindu Marriage Act, the Hindu Succession Act and the Hindu Adoption and Guardianship Act will also cease to be administered by the secular courts. Those who wish to be governed by the Hindu, the Christian or the Muslim law will have to devise their own institutional arrangements for the purpose.

He again argues that Hindu, Muslim, Christian or other personal religious laws should be a matter for the believers to accept without being enforced by the state. Enforcement of religious law should be a private matter, resting solely on the voluntary moral commitment of the parties involved. At the same time, the option of choosing a common code should always be available to all the concerned parties in any domestic dispute. For instance, if a man or a woman feels dissatisfied with the manner in which hislher community administered the personal law in hislher case, the person should be free to approach the civil courts and demand that the provisions of the egalitarian civil code be applicable in their case.

AMBEDKAR ON NATIONALISM: A NATION CALLING FOR A HOME

That there are factors, administrative, linguistic or cultural, which are the predisposing causes behind these demands for separation, is a fact which is admitted and understood by all. Nobody minds these demands and many are prepared to concede them. But, the Hindus say that the Muslims are going beyond the idea of separation and questions, such as what has led them to take this course, why are they asking for partition, for the annulment of the common tie by a legal divorce between Pakistan and Hindustan, are being raised.

The answer is to be found in the declaration made by the Muslim League in its Resolution that the Muslims of India are a separate nation. It is this declaration by the Muslim League, which is both resented and ridiculed by the Hindus.The Hindu resentment is quite natural. Whether India is a nation or not, has been the subject-matter of controversy between the Anglo-Indians and the Hindu politicians ever since the Indian National Congress was founded. The Anglo-Indians were never tired of proclaiming that India was not a nation, that 'Indians' was only another name for the people of India. In the words of one Anglo-Indian "to know India was to forget that there is such a thing as India." The Hindu politicians and patriots have been, on the other hand, equally persistent in their assertion that India is a nation. That the Anglo-Indians were right in their repudiation cannot be gainsaid. Even Dr. Tagore, the national poet of Bengal, agrees with them. But, the Hindus have never yielded on the point even to Dr. Tagore.

This was because of two reasons. Firstly, the Hindu felt ashamed to admit that India was not a nation. In a world where nationality and nationalism were deemed to be special virtues in a people, it was quite natural for the Hindus to feel, to use the language of Mr. H. G. Wells, that it would be as improper for India to be without a nationality as it would be for a man to be without his clothes in a crowded assembly. Secondly, he had realized that nationality had a most intimate connection with the claim for self-government. He knew that by the end of the 19th century, it had become an accepted principle that the people, who constituted a nation, were entitled on that account to self-government and that any patriot, who asked for self-government for his people, had to prove that they were a nation. The Hindu for these reasons never stopped to examine whether India was or was not a nation in fact. He never cared to reason whether nationality was merely a question of calling a people a nation or was a question of the people being a nation. He knew one thing, namely, that if he was to succeed in his demand for self-government for India, he must maintain, even if he could not prove it, that India was a nation.

In this assertion, he was never contradicted by any Indian. The thesis was so agreeable that even serious Indian students of history came forward to write propagandist literature in support of it, no doubt out of patriotic motives. The Hindu social reformers, who knew that this was a dangerous delusion, could not openly contradict this thesis. For, anyone who questioned it was at once called a tool of the British bureaucracy and enemy of the country. The Hindu politician was able to propagate his view for a long time. His opponent, the Anglo-Indian, had ceased to reply to him. His propaganda had almost succeeded. When it was about to succeed comes this declaration of the Muslim League— this rift in the lute. Just because it does not come from the Anglo-Indian, it is a deadlier blow. It destroys the work which the Hindu politician has done for years. If the Muslims in India are a separate nation, then, of course, India is not a nation. This assertion cuts the whole ground from under the feet of the Hindu politicians. It is natural that they should feel annoyed at it and call it a stab in the back.

But, stab or no stab, the point is, can the Musalmans be said to constitute a nation? Everything else is beside the point. This raises the question : What is a nation? Tomes have been written on the subject. Those who are curious may go through them and study the different basic conceptions as well as the different aspects of it. It is, however, enough to know the core of the subject and that can be set down in a few words. Nationality is a social feeling. It is a feeling of a corporate sentiment of oneness which makes those who are charged with it feel that they are kith and kin. This national feeling is a double edged feeling. It is at once a feeling of fellowship for one's own kith and kin and an anti-fellowship feeling for those who are not one's own kith and kin. It is a feeling of "consciousness of kind" which on the one hand binds together those who have it, so strongly that it over-rides all differences arising out of economic conflicts or social gradations and, on the other, severs them from those who are not of their kind. It is a longing not to belong to any other group. This is the essence of what is called a nationality and national feeling.

Now apply this test to the Muslim claim. Is it or is it not a fact that the Muslims of India are an exclusive group? Is it or is it not a fact that they have a consciousness of kind? Is it or is not a fact that every Muslim is possessed by a longing to belong to his own group and not to any non-Muslim group?

If the answer to these questions is in the affirmative, then the controversy must end and the Muslim claim that they are a nation must be accepted without cavil.

What the Hindus must show is that notwithstanding some differences, there are enough affinities between Hindus and Musalmans to constitute them into one nation, or, to use plain language, which make Muslims and Hindus long to belong together.

Hindus, who disagree with the Muslim view that the Muslims are a separate nation by themselves, rely upon certain features of Indian social life which seem to form the bonds of integration between Muslim society and Hindu society.

In the first place, it is said that there is no difference of race between the Hindus and the Muslims. That the Punjabi Musalman and the Punjabi Hindu, the U. P. Musalman and the U. P. Hindu, the Bihar Musalman and the Bihar Hindu, the Bengal Musalman and the Bengal Hindu, the Madras Musalman and the Madras Hindu, and the Bombay Musalman and the Bombay Hindu are racially of one stock. Indeed there is more racial affinity between the Madras Musalman and the Madras Brahmin than there is between the Madras Brahmin and the Punjab Brahmin. In the second place, reliance is placed upon linguistic unity between Hindus and Muslims. It is said that the Musalmans have no common language of their own which can mark them off as a linguistic group separate from the Hindus. On the contrary, there is a complete linguistic unity between the two. In the Punjab, both Hindus and Muslims speak Punjabi. In Sind, both speak Sindhi. In Bengal, both speak Bengali. In Gujarat, both speak Gujarati. In Maharashtra, both speak Marathi. So in every province. It is only in towns that the Musalmans speak Urdu and the Hindus the language of the province. But outside, in the mofussil, there is complete linguistic unity between Hindus and

Musalmans. Thirdly, it is pointed out that India is the land which the Hindus and Musalmans have now inhabited together for centuries. It is not exclusively the land of the Hindus, nor is it exclusively the land of the Mahomedans.

Reliance is placed not only upon racial unity but also upon certain common features in the social and cultural life of the two communities. It is pointed out that the social life of many Muslim groups is honeycombed with Hindu customs. For instance, the Avans of the Punjab, though they are nearly all Muslims, retain Hindu names and keep their genealogies in the Brahmanic fashion. Hindu surnames are found among Muslims. For instance, the surname Chaudhari is a Hindu surname but is common among the Musalmans of U.P. and Northern India. In the matter of marriage, certain groups of Muslims are Muslims in name only. They either follow the Hindu form of the ceremony alone, or perform the ceremony first by the Hindu rites and then call the Kazi and have it performed in the Muslim form. In some sections of Muslims, the law applied is the Hindu Law in the matter of marriage, guardianship and inheritance. Before the Shariat Act was passed, this was true even in the Punjab and the N. W. F. P. In the social sphere the caste system is alleged to be as much a part of Muslim society as it is of Hindu society. In the religious sphere, it is pointed out that many Muslim *pirs* had Hindu disciples; and similarly some Hindu *yogis* have had Muslim *chelas*. Reliance is placed on instances of friendship between saints of the rival creeds. At Girot, in the Punjab, the tombs of two ascetics, Jamali Sultan and Diyal Bhawan, who lived in close amity during the early part of the nineteenth century, stand close to one another, and are reverenced by Hindus and Musalmans alike. Bawa Fathu, a Muslim saint, who lived about 1700 A.D. and whose tomb is at Ranital in the Kangra District, received the title of prophet by the blessing of a Hindu saint, Sodhi Guru Gulab Singh. On the otherhand, Baba Shahana, a Hindu saint whose cult is observed in the Jang District, is said to have been the *chela* of a Muslim *pir* who changed the original name (Mihra), of his Hindu follower, into Mir Shah.

All this, no doubt, is true. That a large majority of the Muslims belong to the same race as the Hindus is beyond question. That all Mahomedans do not speak a common tongue, that many speak the same language as the Hindus cannot be denied. That there are certain social customs which are common to both cannot be gainsaid. That certain religious rites and practices are common to both is also a matter of fact. But the question is: can all this support the conclusion that the Hindus and the Mahomedans on account of them constitute one nation or these things have fostered in them a feeling that they long to belong to each other?

There are many flaws in the Hindu argument. In the first place, what are pointed out as common features are not the result of a conscious attempt to adopt and adapt to each other's ways and manners to bring about social fusion. On the other hand, this uniformity is the result of certain purely mechanical causes. They are partly due to incomplete conversions. In a land like India, where the majority of the Muslim population has been recruited from caste and out-caste Hindus, the Muslimization of the convert was neither complete nor effectual, either from fear of revolt or because of the method of persuasion or insufficiency of preaching due to insufficiency of priests. There is, therefore, little wonder if great sections of the Muslim community here and there reveal their Hindu origin in their religious and social life. Partly it is to be explained as the effect of common environment to which both Hindus and Muslims have been subjected for centuries. A common environment is bound to produce common reactions, and reacting constantly in the same way to the same environment is bound to produce a common type. Partly are these common features to be explained as the remnants of a period of religious amalgamation between the Hindus and the Muslims inaugurated by the Emperor Akbar, the result of a dead past which has no present and no future.As to the argument based on unity of race, unity of language and inhabiting a common country, the matter stands on a different footing. If these considerations were decisive in making or unmaking a nation, the Hindus would be right in saying that by reason of race, community of language and habitat the Hindus and Musalmans form one nation. As a matter of historical experience, neither race, nor language, nor country has sufficed to mould a people into a nation. The argument is so well put by Renan that it is impossible to improve upon his language. Long ago in his famous essay on Nationality, Renan observed :—

"that race must not be confounded with nation. The truth is that . there is no pure race; and that making politics depend upon ethnographical analysis, is allowing it to be borne upon a chimera . . . .Racial facts, important as they are in the beginning, have a constant tendency to lose their importance. Human history is essentially different from zoology. Race is not everything, as it is in the sense of rodents and felines."

Speaking about language, Renan points out that :—

"Language invites re-union; it does not force it. The United States and England, Spanish America and Spain speak the same languages and do not form single nations. On the contrary, Switzerland which owes her stability to the fact that she was founded by the assent of her several parts counts three or four languages. In man there is something superior to language, —will. The will of Switzerland to be united, in spite of the variety of her languages, is a much more important fact than a similarity of language, often obtained by persecution."

Chapter 6

CONTRIBUTION OF DR.B. R. AMBEDKAR TO THE MODERN INDIA

Dr. B.R Ambedkar was among the most outstanding intellectuals of India in the 20th century in the best sense of the word. Hewas a leading activist and social reformer who gave his life functioning for the upliftment of the Dalits and the socially unwilling class of India. A messiah for the oppressed, he continuously fought for eradicationof caste discrimination that had fragmented the Indian society and made it cripple. Born in a socially backward family, Ambedkar was the victim of caste discrimination, inequality and prejudice. However, fighting all odds, he attained higher education thus he became the first ever untouchable to attain the same. No sooner after completinghis higher studies, he launched himself politically fighting for the rights of the depressed class and inequality practiced in the society. He was an advocator of social equality and justice. Academically trained as a jurist, he went on to become the first Law Minister of Independent India and the framer or chief architect of the Constitution of India. He laid special emphasis on dignity, unity, freedom, and rights for all citizens as enshrined in the constitution. Ambedkar advocated democracy in every field social, economic, political. For him social justice meant maximum happiness to the maximum number of people.Birth and Education Bhim Rao was born on 14 April 1891 in an untouchable 'Mahar' family at Mhow, near Indore in the present Madhya Pradesh. He was the fourteenth child of Ramji

Sakpal and Bhimbai. Ramji Sakpal(1848-1913) was a head master in the Military School in the rank of subedar-major. Bhimabai (1854-96) belonged to a well to do family of Murbadkars who were also employed in the British army. Bhimrao's family hailed originally fiom the Ambavade village located in the Ratnagiri District of the present Maharashtra. His official name in the school register was Bhima Rao Ambavadekar. There was a Brahamin teacher in his school with the surname Ambedkar, who somehow had a soft corner for the boy. It was the kindness of this teacher which made him ultimately adopt Ambedkar as his surname. Ambedkar got married to Ramabai, a nine years old girl, at the age of fourteen. He passed matriculation in 1907. With the help of a scholarship offered by Maharaja Syajirao Gaekwad of Baroda, he completed the B.A. degree in 1912. His higher education was in the West. There also his studies were financed by the Maharaja, on an agreement to serve in the Baroda state after completing the studies. He took his MA degree in 19 15 and Ph.D.degree in 1916 from the renowned Columbia University, New York. After successful completion of his studies at the Columbia University he left New York for London and entered the Gray's Inn for doing Bar-at-Law and simultaneously enrolled himself in the London School of Economic and Political Science. But, when he was half the way through his studies the Maharaja of Baroda called him back, as the period of scholarship granted to him was over. Back in India he assumed the office of the Military Secretary to the Maharaja. But due to the unbearable humiliation he had to suffer at the hands of caste-Hindus he left Baroda state. For a shortwhile he worked as a professor of political economy at the Sydenham College, Bombay. He resigned from this post to resume his economic and legal studies in London. This time the Maharaja of Kohlapur rendered him financial assistance. Before leaving for London he had given evidence before the South borough Commission on franchise; and had advocated separate electorate for the untouchables. In 1921 he got his M.Sc. for his thesis ''Provincial Decentralization of Imperial Finance in British India" He obtained the D.S.C.(Econ) degree in 1922 from the London University for the thesis."The Problem of the Rupee: It s Origin and its Solution". Taking his Bar-at-Law degree from the Gray's Inn he went to Germany and joined the famous University of Bonn for a higher course of studies in economics. But he could not complete his studies due to shortage of funds. Dr. Ambedkar as a social reformer Dr. Ambedkar believed in peaceful methods of social change. He was supported to constitutional lines in the evolutionary process of social transformation. He thought the factors like law and order which are indispensable for social life. It also strives to sustain institutions that will make better „social order . He was opposite to the aggressive me thodin communal change for it obstruction the composure and create chaos. He had no faith in anarchy methods. A welfare state of all cannot be developed on the grounds of terror, force and brutal methods. According to him violent method to a peaceable cultureis not only in appropriate but too irrational and immoral.He was a true Renaissance man, a person who excelled in many different areas of inquiry. Though he was hated by conventional Hindus and labelled as a demolisher of Hinduism, historians now realize the crucial role Dr. Ambedkar played in recognizing Hindu society. Far from being a traitor, he played an important role in revitalizing Hinduism, reviving it by challenging everything that was unjust and unfair within it. In fact, he brought about a renaissance of Hinduism by provoking the Hindus to rethink some of the basic tenets of their religion. Dr. Ambedkar had a great faith in social reformers to create public opinion for against of the gross inequalities in the society. He urged them to found organizations to deal with urgent cases of discrimination.

The organizations should deal the powerful section of society to give a chance to the oppressed and depressed classes to work in different sectors. The Hindu society should give a space to depressed sections by employing them in their various sectors suited to the capacities of applicants.

According to him, social change and social justice are indeed critical to the egalitarianism that any democracy must aspire it. As a social democrat Dr. Ambedkar worried on a much broader view of steady rebuilding of country with comprehensive expansion and cultural integration in the Nation without caste discrimination. As the major architect of the Indian constitution, Dr. Ambedkar constructed the safeguards for establishing a more equitable society to millions of oppressed and depressed classes. He was strongly believed that political institutions were responsible for reforming the existing social institutions by using legislative force to yield the results. Political institutions will survive only when they actively work for social reformation. Dr. Ambedkar was a freedom fighter of the truest kind, not merely dreaming of setting India force from British rule, but of transforming India into a country where freedom holds meaning for everyone. While Mahatma Gandhi led fellow Indians in a struggle against discrimination in South Africa, Dr. Ambedkar led a battle, too, against prejudice within his own country. By securing equality for his community, he was creating a more equal world for us all.

Dr. Ambedkar as an Educationist

Dr. Ambedkar considered education as a powerful instrument for raising the overall status of the depressed and deprived classes. He thought, It is education that furnishes moral arsenal for any social movement, the more education the more the chances for progress. In his struggle for the liberation of the Dalits from the Hindu social slavery, Ambedkar had the right cognizance of the role that education has to play. He desired the elevation of the depressed classes to be the responsibility of the enlightened people in the country. Thus he established a chain of schools colleges and hostels under the shield of the People's Education Society whichhe had founded in 1945. His emphasis, however, does not rest merely on academic education. He had realised the importance of mass education. Accordingly he conceived education as a means to make the Dalits aware of their social realities and to develop in them courage and commitment to fight casteism. He published four periodicals namely 'Mooknayak' (1920), 'Bahishkrit Bharat' (1927), 'Samatha' (1929) and 'Janata' (1930). He exhorted his followers that 'it is disgraceful to live at the cost of one's self respect and it is out of hard and 4 ceaseless struggle alone one derives strength, confidence and recognition . His career as teacher, principal and member of legislative enabled him to get insight into the academic and administrative problems of higher education, it also provided him rich experience and knowledge of the complexities of educational concerns. He urged the teachers and the educated parents to meet the requirements and challenges of the modern world and called on them to work for inculcation of rational thinking and scientific temper among the masses in general and the young generation in particular. To him, education is the only right weapon to cut down social slavery. It will enlighten the dalits to achieve elevated social status, economic betterment and human and political rights. It would enhance adjournment of the age old values and would inculcate the values required for a pluralist society. It is out of this conviction that he made 'educate' the first word of his slogan "Educate, Agitate, Organise".

As a Warrior against Casteism

Ambedkar's birth in an 'untouchable' community made him undergo humiliating experiences. In those days untouchability was deeply entrenched in the minds of the caste Hindus. Ambedkar fought the caste-ridden unjust society on all fronts-social, religious, political and economic. His encounter with casteism and untouchability opened a new course in the social reform movement in India. Unlike the earlier reformers who limited the cause of social progress and welfare within a general frame of reference, Ambedkar concentrated his power and resources on the cause of liberationof a particular section, the Dalits. Ambedkar's ideological conflict ith the Hindu social order and casteism developed into direct action in March 1924 when a meeting of the untouchables was convened at the Damodar Hall,

Bombay. The foundation of" Bahishkrit Hitakarini Sabha" set a concrete platform to represent the grievances of the depressed classes. Duringthe early phase of his movement Ambedkar demanded equal rights particularly social and religious, for the Dalits. But later the association set importance extraon the political rights of the depressed classes. Ambedkar no more fought within the fabric of Hinduism. While the congress boycotted the Simon Commission he did not hesitate to tender evidence before it on behalf of the Dalits. He felt that it was his duty to promote their interests by demanding separate electorates. O n this matter he had to confront with Gandhiji in the Second Round Table Conference. Ambedkar formed the Independent Labour Party (1LP) topromote the cause of the depressed classes. When, under the Government of India Act 1935, election to the provincial legislatures was declared, his party contested the election in seventeen seats in the Bombay Presidency and won fifteen. However, congress formed the government and Ambedkar joined the opposition. A notable achievement of his party in the legislature was the introduction of the bill for abolition of Mahar Watan and K hoti. The bill was aimed at liquidating the feudal land tenure system that prevailed in the Konkan region. As a member of the constituent assembly and as chairman of the Draft Committee of Indian Constitution, Ambedkardid his best to safeguard the interests of the depressed classes. The constitution established a uniform or single system of citizenship law for the country. It outlawed the stigma of untouchability and prohibited discrimination on the ground of religion,caste, race and sex. There are provisions in the Constitution for protecting the political rights of the depressed sections of the society.

Ambedkar as an eminent economist

Dr. Ambedkar work in economics is noteworthy. His views deals with public finance and agriculture are landmark in the economics. Prof. A. K. Sen has also said, "Ambedkar is my Father in Economics. He is factual celebrated champion of the disadvantaged. He deserve additiona lthan what he has achieve today.His contribution in the field of economics is splendid and will be remembered forever..!"Ambedkar said,,,Economy in public expenditure does not simply mean a low level of public spending, but it is the cleveruse of finances so that every paisa fetches the most benefit. Those in charge of public funds must strive to evaluate alternative methods of achieving the objectives and see to it that leakages do not occur. Ambedkar s commitment was internal stability and he was convinced that only an automatic system based on gold standard with gold currency could achieve this desirable end. He was of view that governments should spend the resources garnered from the public not only as per rules, laws and regulations, but also to see that "faithfulness, wisdom and economy". Over ruling in a conversation in the Bombay Legislative Council on October 10, 1927, Dr. Ambedkar argued that the solution to the agrarian question "lies not in increasing the size of farms, but in having concentrated cultivation that is employing additional capital and more labour on the farms such as we have." Further on, he says: "The better method is to begin cooperative agriculture and to compel owner of little flooring to join in cultivation." Thus Ambedkar thought on public Finance and agriculture has vital relevance and still applicable in current situation of India. In command to improve out put of agriculture sector, government is needed to take measures on the basis of Dr. Ambedkar s consideration. In his work 'State and Minorities' he suggested to bring all the key and basic industries as well as agriculture and insurances beneath the manag eof State monopoly. He also postulated that the State should divide the acquired agricultural land into farms of standard sizes and let these out to farmers without any consideration of caste and creed. The worth of his conclusion is consider able exactly since his analysis was based on sound empirical and historical foundations. Key industries shall be own and run by the state. Basic but non-key industries shall be owned by the condition and run by the state or by corporation recognized by it. Agriculture shall be a state industry, and be organized by the state taking over all land and letting it out for cultivation in suitable standard sizes to residents of villages; these shall be cultivated as group farms by groups of families. He also stresses the need for industrialization so as to shift extra labour from agriculture to previous creative occupation, accompanied by large capital investments in agriculture to raise yields. He sees an extremely important role for the state in such transformation of agriculture and advocates the nationalization of land and the leasing out of land to groups of cultivators, who are to be confident to form cooperatives in order to promote agriculture. He was a believer in state socialism which he upheld as essential for the rapid industrialization of India.

REFERENCES

1. Arnbedkar, B.R. - "All-India Radio Broadcast Speech" on October 3, 1954.
2. latava, D. R. - "The Philosophy of Dr. Ambedkar" from 'The Emancipator of the oppressed', edited by K.N. Kadam, 1993.
3. Ambedkar, B.R. - "States and Minorities", pp.32. [Thacker and Co Ltd, Bombay, 1947.]
4. Ibid. pp.33-4.
5. Ambedkar, B.R. - "Pakistan or Partition of India", pp. 298.
6. Ibid., pp. 300.
7. Constituent Assembly Debates, Vol. VII, pp. 535.
8. Kuber, W. N. - "Ambedkar", (PPH, New Delhi, 1973), pp. 200.
9. Keer, op. cit., pp. 488.
10. Ambedkar, B.R. - "Congress and Gandhi"(Thacker and Co Ltd, Bombay, 1945), pp. 296.
11. Ambedkar, B.R. - "States and Minorities" pp. 3.
12. Ambedkar, B.R. - "Ranade, Gandhi and linnah"(Address delivered on the 10 I 5t Birth Celebration of Ranade: Thacker and Co Ltd, Bombay, 1943.), pp. 36.
13. Ambedkar, B.R. - "Annihilation of Caste", (1935), pp. 38.
14. . CA Debates, VoL XI, pp.979.
15. Ibid.

16. Ibid.

17. Ibid., VoLVn, pp. 494.

18. Ambedkar, Address to AITU Camp, Delhi, 17 September 1948.

19. Ambedkar, B.R. - "Writings and Speeches", VolA, (Compiled by Vasant Moon), pp. 286-87.

20. B.R. - "Annihilation of Caste", pp. 34.

21. Mangudkar, M.P. - "Why Dr. Ambedkar was not a Communist?" [From 'The Emancipator of the Oppressed', edited by K.N. Kadam), pp. 168.

22. Ibid., pp. 172-3.

23. Biswas, Oneil- "A Phenomenon named Ambedkar", (1998), pp.244.

24. The Times of India, Bombay, 21 March, 1940.

25. Ramaswamy, k. - "Ambedkar: A True Democrat and Nationalist", from' Ambedkar and Nation-building' edited by S. Lal and K.S. Saxena.

26. Ambedkar, B.R. - "Case for Hindu Code" (1949), pp.l2.

27. Tiwari, Y.K. - "Ambedkar's Vision of Uniform Civil Code", from 'Ambedkar and Nation-building', edited by Shyam Lal and K.S. Saxena.

28. CAD, Vol.Vn (1948), pp. 781.

29. Ahir, D.C. - "Ambedkar and Indian Constitution", pp. 134-35.

30. Thorat, S.K. - "Ambedkar's Thought on Economic Development and Planning", from 'Ambedkar and Nation-building' Edited by S. Lal and K.S. Saxena. pp.85.

31. Ibid., pp.87.

32. Ambedkar's address to the session of the All-India Scheduled Castes Federation, Bombay, May 6, 1945.

33. Ambedkar, B.R. - "The Buddha and His Dhamma", (People's Education Society, Bombay, 1957), pp.317.

34. The Andhra Republican of 5th September 1965, edited by Endluri.

35. Omvedt, Gail - "Ambedkar", (2004), pp. 74.

36. Janata, 15 January 1938, edited by Ambedkar.

37. Kshirsagar, R.K. - "The Political Parties Founded by Dr. Babasaheb Ambedkar", from 'Dr. B.R. Ambedkar', edited by K.N. Kadam, pp. 159-60.

38. Rattu, Nanak Chand - "Last Few Years of Dr. Ambedkar", (New Delhi, 1997), pp. 45.

39. Jaffrelot, Christophe - "Dr. Ambedkar and Untouchability" (New Delhi, 2005), pp. 74.

40. Duncan, R.I. - "Levels, the Communication of Programmes and Sectional Strategies in Indian Politics", (University of Sussex, 1979), pp. 214.

41. Zelliot, E. - "Learning the Use of Political Means", in R. Kothari (ed.), Caste in Indian Politics, New Delhi, 1970, pp. 50.

42. Ambedkar, B.R. - "Writings and Speeches", Vol.2, pp. 90.

43. Quoted in G. Omvedt, Dalits and Democratic Revolution, (New Delhi, 1994), pp. 197-98.

44. Ambedkar, B.R. - "Writings and Speeches", Vol.2, op. cit., pp. 201-32.

45. Zelliot, E. - "Dr. Ambedkar", University of Pennsylvania, 1969, pp.25.

46. Keer, D. - "Dr. Ambedkar", pp. 480.

47. Jaffrelot, Christophe - "Dr. Ambedkar and Untouchability" (2005), pp.79-80.

48. Moon, V. - "Growing up Untouchable in India", pp.66.

49. Jaffrelot, Christophe - "Dr. Ambedkar and Untouchability", op. cit., pp. 80.

50. Ambedkar, B.R. - 'Objections to Cripps proposals, App. IX to What Congress and Gandhi have done to the Untouchables', Dr, Babasaheb Ambedkar, *Writings and Speeches,* Bombay, Govt. of Maharashtra, Vol. 9, pp. 339.

51. Ibid., pp. 353.

52. Cited in B. Nicholas, "Below the Bottom Rung"; a British Estimate of Dr. Ambedkar, 1944, in K.C. Yadav, *From Periphery to Centre Stage,* pp.47.

53. The Ti~es of India, 24 Sept. 1944.

54. Cited in *The Hindu* (Madras), 26 September 1944.

55. Cited in The Liberator, 26 Sept. 1944.

56. Ibid., 24 Sept. 1944.

57. P.D. Reeves, B.D. Graham and *1.M.* Goodman, Elections in UP, 1920-51, New Delhi; Manohar, 1975, pp. 315-19.

58. ZeUiot, E. - "Learning the use of Political means", op. cit., pp.53.

59. Bandyopadhyay, S. - "Transfer of Power and the crisis of Dalit Politics in India, 1945-

60. 47", Modern Indian Studies, 34(4),2000, pp. 913.

61. Zelliot, E. - "Dr. Ambedkar", op. cit., pp. 265.

62. 1affrelot, C. - "Dr. Ambedkar and Untouchability", op. cit., pp. 84.

63. Duncan, J. -"Levels, the Communication of Programmes and Sectional Strategies in Indian Politics", op. cit., pp.236.

64. 1affrelot, C. - "Dr. Ambedkar and Untouchability", op. cit., pp. 86.

65. Gokhale, *1.* - "From Concessions to Confrontation", *The Politics of an Indian Untouchable Community,* Bombay, 1993, pp.217.

66. Election Manifesto of the Scheduled Castes Federation, SeE 1957, pp. 14 (Ambedkar papers, NMML, Section of microfilms, Reel no. 2.)

67. 1affrelot, C. - "Dr. Ambedkar and Untouchability", op. cit., pp. 88.

68. Pai, Suclha - "Reorganization of States", in 'Ambedkar in Retrospect', Edited by Sukhadeo Thorat & Aryama, New Delhi, 2007, pp. 196-7.

69. States Reorganization Commission, Manager of Publications, Government of India, 1955: 35.

70. Pai, Sudha - "Reorganization of States", op. cit., pp. 199-202.

71. Later published as "Thoughts on Linguistic States" in Speeches and Writings Baba Saheb Ambedkar, Vol. 1, Education Department, Government of Maharashtra, 1979, pp. 99-128.

72. Pai, Sudha- "Reorganization of States", op. cit., pp. 202.

73. Ambedkar, B.R. - "Thoughts on Linguistic States", op. cit., pp. 169.

74. Published in Times oflndia, 23 April, 1953.

75. Pai, Sudha - "Reorganization of states", op. cit., pp. 204-6.

76. Rodrigües, Valerian - "Good Society: Rights, Democracy and Socialism", in 'Ambedkar in Retrospect', edited by S. Thorat and Aryama, 2007, pp. 144.

77. Ambedkar, B.R. - "Writings and Speeches", Vol. 3, part II, India and Prerequisites of Communism, pp. 95-6, Bombay, Government of Maharashtra.

78. Rodrigues, Valerian - "Good Society: Rights, Democracy and Socialism", in 'Ambedkar in Retrospect'(2007), edited by S. Thorat and Aryama, pp. 145-46.

79. McMillan, Alistair - "Standing at the Margins: Representation and Electoral Reservation in India" (2005), Oxford University Press, New-Delhi, pp. 95.

80. Baxi, Upendra - "Ambedkar Memorial Lecture" (1978), University of Madras, pp. 10.

81. Cited in A. Gajendran, 'Representation', (2007), op. cit., pp. 188.